Lessons from Lorena

Kimberly J. Stults

Lessons from Lorena

Living with Autism

TATE PUBLISHING & Enterprises

Published by Tate Publishing & Enterprises, LLC
127 E. Trade Center Terrace | Mustang, Oklahoma 73064 USA
1.888.361.9473 | www.tatepublishing.com

Tate Publishing is committed to excellence in the publishing industry. The company reflects the philosophy established by the founders, based on Psalm 68:11,
"The Lord gave the word and great was the company of those who published it."

Book design copyright © 2010 by Tate Publishing, LLC. All rights reserved.
Cover design by Amber Gulilat
Interior design by Joel Uber

Published in the United States of America

ISBN: 978-1-61739-079-1
1. Family & Relationships / Learning Disabilities
2. Self-Help / Motivational & Inspirational
10.09.20

In memory of my mom.
In honor of my dad.

Table of Contents

Introduction

Our family had five Michaels: my grandpa, uncle, cousin, dad, and brother. When I was introduced to my husband, Mike, on a blind date, I knew my fate was sealed. We were married on October 17, 1987. Our son, the seventh Michael (Mickey), came into our family on February 4, 1990. I liked the sense of history and connection to family through a name, so when our daughter arrived the next year in August, we decided to give her a family name too. We named her Lorena, after my great-grandma Swope. Grandma Swope was a large woman whose heart outsized her body. She was famous for her baking and her love. I couldn't think of a better legacy for a child.

I see the reflection of our family in both my children. They both have my mom's full, perfectly proportioned lips. We tease Mickey about his inheritance of his Grandpa Ruffing's butt. I am sure my husband looks at them and sees his own family reflections. Lorena has his generous forehead, which came from his dad. Most of all, though, I see myself in them.

Friends and family often observe that, "Mickey acts just like you," to my amusement and his typical teenage disgust. They also observe, "Oh my God, Lorena could be your twin." I know what they mean. I look at her, and it is like looking in a mirror and seeing my younger self. Too bad it isn't that easy to peel away the years. Yet there is one major difference between Lorena and the rest of the family. Lorena is autistic.

I had always thought that as the parent I would be the teacher, coach, and guide. Silly, silly woman. I didn't realize that by becoming a parent I was to become the student as well. And that by having an autistic child my life would have an unexpected dimension that would teach me the most important lessons of my life.

Lorena has given me the chance to experience life in a different way. I did not choose this path. She often leads me down it unwillingly. Yet I recognize that these lessons are a bittersweet gift, which includes moments of the deepest pain and the greatest joy. I believe I am not the only person who benefits from these lessons. I see her impact on friends, family, colleagues, and even strangers. Many of these people have encouraged me to share Lorena's lessons, and so this book was born.

Armageddon

Armageddon is one of my favorite movies. Now, if you haven't seen it and still want to, you might want to skip the next couple of paragraphs. Of course, you might not be able to figure out what I am talking about at that point, but hey, life is full of choices. In *Armageddon*, an earth-killing meteor is heading toward earth. It is Bruce Willis's character's job to take his band of misfits into outer space and save the earth by blowing up the meteor. Of course, at the crucial moment when they are supposed to leave the meteor, the bomb's timer fails. That leaves Bruce behind to set off the bomb at the cost of his own life. As the meteor is exploding around him, his life with his daughter flashes before his eyes.

I identify with Bruce in that moment. My own armageddon began the week before my daughter's birth in August 1991. That is when I got the early morning phone call that my Grandma Gerber was being taken to the emergency room after passing out in the yard. I was Grandma and Grandpa's first grandchild. They doted on me. Each of their four children, nine grandchildren, and one great-grandchild made that identical claim. There was nothing better for them than when all the "kids" came home. It didn't matter that you were completely grown, maybe lived in a different state, had your own home, and your own kids—when you came to their house, you were going home.

Grandma Gerber had suffered a stroke the previous November, and *suffered* was the correct word. She battled the effects. It was disheartening for the entire family to watch this vibrant woman's mental capacities diminish. Her family still brought her incredible joy, though, and she had been waiting impatiently for her second great-grandchild to be born. For three weeks before her hospitalization, every time I called her she was sure I was telling her the baby had arrived and was disgusted when that wasn't the purpose of the call. Instead, it was my grandma who went to the hospital and in the ensuing days, lost her final fight with her illness.

She was still typical Grandma right to the end. She was intubated—had a tube in her throat to her lungs—to help her breathe, yet she was mouthing words right around the tube. Every time I walked in the room—and it was quite an entrance because I was hugely pregnant, overdue by the doctor's calculations—she would mouth the word *baby*. I would shake my head. "Not yet, Grandma." The next word was as clear as if she had spoken it, and it was not a word said in polite company. You could just see her frustration; she wanted me to deliver. Unfortunately, that event did not happen before my grandma's death. My beloved grandma died five days before my daughter's birth.

My daughter was born on August 7, 1991. Unlike Bruce, my past life did not pass before my eyes, but my future vision of it did. I saw Lorena's future ballet lessons, that first day of kindergarten, her first bra, mother-daughter shopping trips, fights over clothes and piercings, her graduation, and, of course, her inauguration. Hey, I had big dreams, but this girl would have all the opportunities the world had to offer. Who knew that before the year was out that vision would be blown up as surely as the meteor in *Armageddon*?

The days after Lorena's birth are blurry. I was exhausted mentally and physically. Grandma Gerber's funeral was overwhelming and frustrating. I was afraid that I would go into labor and not be able to attend. I could tell that people were trying to protect me in my "delicate" condition, although, as previously mentioned, I was as big as a Clydesdale horse. People would progress through the obligatory receiving line, offering their condolences, until they reached me. I would get the pregnancy questions: "So, when are you due?" "Do you know what you are having?" "Is Mickey excited about being a big brother?" I realized that they were trying not to upset the pregnant lady and be kind, yet their good intentions made me feel isolated and even more sad.

Daily, I was seeing my physician because, according to the ultrasound, I was quite overdue. We decided that I would be induced the day after the funeral. I was a tornado of conflicting emotions. Mike and I were so excited that our second child was finally coming, yet I was devastated that my grandma was not going to see this little person. I felt guilty that I had not managed to fulfill her last wish to see this great-grandchild. Then, at the end of the day, I felt only exasperation, as my uterus just refused to cooperate. We went home that day, and the next day started the whole cycle of emotions and induction again. Thank God, this time the induction worked.

This joy was quickly followed by one of the most heart-breaking moments. My Grandpa Gerber came to see Lorena. You could just see the devastation on his face. He tried so hard to appear happy, but he just couldn't get there. That roller coaster was what I remember about the next few months—happiness followed by sadness, depression, and even anger.

In late September, I got this rotten cold. I think now that my body was just reacting to all the emotional stress. Unfortunately, I shared this misery with Lorena. My bouncing baby girl spiked fevers, a continuously running nose, ear infections, and a body-racking cough that would just not go away. For a month we ran her to the doctor, sat up with her at night, and tried a variety of antibiotics to treat her. Again, in hindsight, I realize that she had RSV (respiratory syncytial virus), a respiratory viral infection that has a very negative impact on a little body. I watched this impact on my baby girl. Lorena seemed to shrink before my eyes. She grew longer but did not gain weight. I look at pictures of her at three months; she is plump and animated. By Christmas, four months after her birth, she was limp, without facial expression, and holding her arms in funny positions with wrists flexed and turned inward.

I am a nurse, and these symptoms started to ring little alarm bells in my mind, yet the mother in me denied the seriousness of these signs. She was really sick, but she would recover. Yet, as time went on, my nurse alarm system picked up other cues. She didn't reach for objects like babies do. It was hard work to get her to smile. She was sensitive to noises. For example, she would jerk awake at a door lightly being shut. And she was the only baby I knew who hated the baby swing. I swear she got motion sickness from it. She would throw up every time she was in it. I was so depressed and sad about Grandma that I couldn't focus on these alarms. I just didn't have enough emotional energy to deal with my grief and these bewildering facts.

Christmas was especially hard that year. I just didn't want to do it. I didn't want to decorate, bake cookies, or shop. I didn't know how we would have Christmas without Grandma. But I did it because I had a two-year-old at home and I knew I had to pull it together for him. In fact, Mickey was my saving grace that season.

He loves music. That year he would grab my hand and say, "Play Christmas songs, Mommy." I would put my favorite Christmas tapes in and then we would "waltz" around the living room. His tiny hands would grab my fingers, and we would twirl around and around. He would grin from ear to ear, and how could you not find the magic of the season in the face of such joy?

Christmas seemed to be a turning point for me. Once we got through the holiday that I had dreaded, I didn't feel so overwhelmed. This was a short reprieve, though. I no longer could turn a deaf ear to those alarms in regards to Lorena. I still blamed those troubling symptoms on her lingering illness. I denied the fact that there might be a bigger problem. I did not share my deepest fears with Mike or my parents. It was easier to hope the fear was unfounded if I didn't voice it out loud.

I did share my fears with our family physician. "She isn't rolling over by herself yet." All health-care personnel learn early in their classes the Denver Developmental list. This list is a guideline based on normal guidelines stating when a child will reach certain milestones. For instance, infants usually roll over by four months, have stranger anxiety at eight months, etc. It is a loose guideline because babies don't read it and therefore, don't always follow the rules. Because I knew that, it gave me ample opportunity to go into denial in regard to Lorena's delays. I distinctly remember sitting and folding laundry one day in the living room. Lorena was sitting in her baby chair and her head wobbled to the side. She was six months old, and I knew she should be able to lift her own head up easily by now. I watched her struggle to do this. Her little neck muscles strained, her head unsteadily bobbing. I silently prayed, "Please let her do it; please let her do it. Don't let anything be wrong." Her head came up. I pushed aside the alarm and fear. *She's just worn out from being sick. She's fine.*

Our physician agreed with me, stating that every baby had his or her own schedule. After all, she had been really ill; we needed to give her time to get better and catch up. The next day, she rolled over. I tucked my fears away.

Occasionally I would casually mention it to my mom. She always reassured me, saying how sick Lorena had been and that she just needed to get better. Only later did Mom relate she had had her own doubts. She shared that when I brought Lorena to the doctor (Mom worked for our family physician) she was concerned because she never grabbed at the paper charts on the desk like all the other babies her age did. Mom would hold her, and Lorena would not play with her necklace. She always had her hands positioned with elbows bent and wrists turned in, which looked awkward and not normal. Mom shared her doubts with Grandpa but tells me now that I was devastated over Grandma and she felt she just couldn't add another blow by expressing her concerns. I can honestly say if she had, I would have flatly denied there was anything wrong, because she was right. I was just not ready to accept the truth.

The truth had a mind of its own and decided to make its presence known with Lorena's hospitalization in March at the age of eight months. Her admission was at our local hospital where I worked. We admitted her because she began again experiencing bronchial spasms with coughing and fever. This hospitalization was the first time our family physician told us he was concerned with Lorena's delays. I was snapped out of denial instantly when he suggested that we needed to have a specialist look at her. "I just want a second opinion." I instantly became tearful and sick to my stomach.

I am a nurse with over twenty years of experience. I had been a nurse for six years when Lorena was born. My entire perception of health care took a 180-degree turn after becoming the patient's family caregiver. Lorena was hospitalized first in my home hospital after a few months of being ill. She was admitted in the evening. I was exhausted. For weeks, Mike and I had been working full time, taking care of Mickey, getting through the holidays, and caring for this very ill child on very little sleep. As I explained, I was grief stricken, but Mike was still grieving the loss of his father, who had died four years before, on Christmas Eve. The holidays were still difficult for him. We had been traveling this bumpy road for months, and the route was about to get more torturous. The road to Lorena's diagnosis was not a straight path. It was full of wrong turns and potholes. We drove blindly into our first pothole when the specialist came to see us that evening.

My good friend and fellow nurse Linda often comments that physicians really should skip that class in medical school called "How to be an SOB 101." Unfortunately, many physicians take it twice. The specialist who came to see Lorena didn't *take* the class; he *taught* it. He was reputed to treat nursing staff and patients as though they had been born without brain tissue. The charge nurse came into the room and told us he was on his way. She looked right at me and said, "I told him that he better understand you are one smart cookie." He didn't get it.

He came swinging into the room, made a very shallow exam, and proceeded to tell us a variety of diagnoses. Poor Mike was horror stricken. My heart was pounding. I know I didn't hear it all because I was so upset, but there are a couple of statements I remember. He told us that with her delays and muscle tone, at worst she could have an anterior horn disorder—a neurological disorder—and if she did, she would continue to degenerate and wouldn't live past the age of five. Then he started talking about muscle biopsies, which would be sent out to Germany. I wish I could say I am exaggerating for literary effect, but I'm not; that is exactly what he said to us. Mike repeats it verbatim. The doctor then told us that at best she was just "floppy" and would need therapy. I remember thinking, *Great, so my best hope is that I have a "floppy" child*. All I could think about was the dog my brother and I had as a kid who had big ears, so we named him Floppy. Now, not only were my worst fears confirmed that my child was not normal, but she might be dying.

We cried. I made phone calls to my aunt, my brother, my mom and dad. I don't even remember what I said. In addition, we did something that as a nurse I had been furious with parents for doing. We went home and left Lorena in that hospital room with the nurses to care for her. I can't tell you how many times I had judged parents because their child was hospitalized and they went home to sleep or out to smoke.

I realize now that while some were not very good parents, the rest were perfectly fine parents. The kind of parents who leave their sick child in the hospital are caring for other children at home, going to work to try to pay the bills, are exhausted, or are just trying to get back to some kind of normalcy. I could not stay in that hospital another minute. I could not care for her that night. I needed to escape to my own home, and I needed to sleep. So we went home. And you know what? My friends—my fellow nurses—cared for her through the night and did a wonderful job. No one judged me when I came back. In fact, they were concerned, asking if I had slept and how I was doing. It was a humbling lesson I will never forget. *Sometimes, you just need to escape to be able to handle what is happening, and it doesn't mean you are a bad parent or person.*

I also did something that as a nurse I had often encouraged families to do, and that was stand up for themselves. I often tell people, "The physician is your employee and you pay him, so you have a right to treatment with respect and dignity." The specialist came in, and I explained to him exactly why his diagnosis could not be accurate. Let's just say that didn't make his day. Okay, I admit it: I really didn't get much sleep. I spent a good deal of the night going through old textbooks from nursing school.

My family physician came in to make morning rounds. I told him that the specialist was not allowed in Lorena's room again and why. My family physician then won my respect forever. He sighed and agreed that he would cancel further consults. He didn't argue with me or stick to the old buddy system. He respected my feelings, and that meant the world to me at that moment. I learned that good doctors listen to and respect their patients. They know it is not about them being superior or right but about the patients getting the care they need.

I learned, on a personal level, how careful you must be with words. I could not get out of my head that unfounded prognosis of Lorena's decline and death. I know Mike thought of it often too. Her first birthday, we bought champagne and celebrated that we got to that milestone. But until her fifth birthday, every cold, every bad night, I would fear that statement would come true. I recall many a morning standing in front of her bedroom door and mouthing a silent prayer that she would be alive and well when I opened that door.

On a spring night, two weeks after the admission in March, I gave Lorena her bath, dressed her in a fluffy pink sleeper, and laid her in the playpen. I went through the same routine with Mickey (except he got blue pajamas; his Dad wasn't secure enough to let me put him in pink). I walked in to check on Lorena and found her pale, limp, and barely breathing. I picked her up and felt her skinny chest retracting with each breath. Again, my personality split. The mother panicked and the nurse assessed. I immediately began a breathing treatment—she had been on them for a while—and dialed 911. I also called my mom. I sat in the chair, cuddling my daughter, praying fervently that she would keep breathing and that the ambulance would hurry.

Mickey picked up on my panic. "Rena okay, Mom?" His anxious little face peered into hers. I tried to reassure him but was not very effective—he threw up on me. In moments, my mom's car screeched into the driveway before the ambulance. After what I swear was one hundred years, the ambulance arrived. The EMS personnel, who were coworkers, took one look, slapped oxygen on her, loaded her and me into the ambulance, and took off with sirens screaming.

I called Mike from the hospital to tell him that Lorena was being transferred to a pediatric hospital. Lorena and I again were loaded into a screaming ambulance and transported to the pediatric hospital. That hospital stay would last one week. Multiple specialists poked, prodded, and tested. That was when the meteor exploded and our personal armageddon occurred.

I have to share how I looked when we arrived at the pediatric hospital. It was my day off, so I was wearing my usual at-home uniform: ratty sweats, a rattier T-shirt, no proper foundation garments, hair standing on end, obviously no makeup, and Mickey's vomit. My dad had gone with Mike to the hospital, while Mickey had gone home with Grandma. The three of us were ushered into a waiting room. I made up my mind in that little room that I was going to hide my light under a basket. I was not going to tell them I was a nurse or argue with the doctor. I was going to keep quiet, be a good little mother, and just find out what was wrong with my baby. The intentions were good, but I just gotta be me. The doctor came in, and he immediately got points for kindness. He explained that more than likely Lorena had a mucous plug, which, between the oxygen, breathing treatment, and suctioning in the ER, was now gone. Her respiratory status was better.

I asked a few questions. He looked at me and said, "You must be a nurse." I thought, *Oh boy, here we go*. We didn't go anywhere. He went to the land of doctor speak, using medical jargon and shorthand explanations. It went right over my head because at that moment, under those circumstances, I wasn't a nurse; I was a mother and needed to be treated as such. Do I sound like a split personality, wanting to be a nurse or mother at a whim? I think back to what my psych teacher taught me in nursing school: you can only be the best you at that moment. Sometimes the best me was a nurse, and sometimes the best me was a mom.

I did understand that Lorena was going to be admitted to their step-down unit. The rules and regulations of the step-down unit horrified me. We were not allowed to stay with her between the hours of nine p.m. and nine a.m.—absolutely no one—and they had security to make sure parents left. Every night, all the parents of these hospitalized children would load into the elevator. Then those who could not cry in front of others would comfort those who could. I decided that the intent of this rule was probably so parents could rest, but it didn't work. We drove the hour home and woke up after a few hours of fitful sleep to make multiple phone calls to the nurses' station, where we were informed by nurses who were clearly not pleased with the interruptions that "she was fine." Now, this seems to contradict my earlier revelation in regard to parents leaving, but in my opinion, parents should be able to stay or leave according to their needs. Are they sometimes not in touch with their needs? Yes, but that is what a caring, collaborative nurse-patient relationship is for: to encourage parents to take care of themselves.

I felt that the other purpose of this rule was so the physicians could poke and prod our children without the parents' presence and pesky questions. I still am not entirely positive how many doctors or what kinds saw Lorena during that stay. Each doctor made rounds before nine a.m. I found the nurses to be reluctant to discuss findings, which frankly ticked me off. Lorena had an MRI, and we didn't even know it was scheduled. I demanded to see a doctor. The neurologist came in, told us that he wasn't sure exactly what was wrong (I did appreciate not having the list of possible diagnoses again), what tests would be run, and discussed therapy she would undergo when she was discharged. He also told us that she would be discharged the next day, after seven days in the hospital. I think I was more excited about bringing her home this time than after she was born.

The next day did not go as planned, however. My dad and I arrived at nine a.m. The doctor did not write the discharge order. The nurses called the resident down. The resident wouldn't write the order. I began to ask questions about tests and lab results. He wouldn't give me straight answers and promised the attending would be in soon. Hours went by and my temper grew.

One of the residents on Lorena's team made the mistake of walking down the hall, and I chased. I cornered him in the exam room. My dad was right behind me. I demanded to see her chart and to see it now. I told him I was sick of not getting information or seeing a real doctor. I want you to know he really was a nice young man, but I had reached my limit. He tried to talk, and I told him to stand in a corner and shut up. I told him I knew it was my right to see her chart, and I wanted to see it now and have some answers. He brought it in and started to read it to me. I just grabbed it and looked for what I wanted. MRI, nothing conclusive; Upper Airway Exam, normal; labs, normal; Gastric pH, normal. We really didn't have any answer except for what she didn't have and the fact that the EEG was pending. And that is why they wouldn't discharge her, because her EEG was pending.

The resident's boss came in and told me we could leave, but it would be AMA (against medical advice), and I had been told that the insurance company wouldn't pay the bill if you left AMA. I told him that. I'll never forget the look on his face, like I was some crazed woman who was a pain in the butt. And I was, but circumstances had created this monster. He must have made some calls, though, because the attending came in shortly. He began by apologizing. "I'm sorry I took so long, but I have had a really bad day." His face hung forlornly. I looked right at him. "I really don't care. All I care about is getting home." He didn't look forlorn anymore.

My philosophy of nursing is caring for the patient as a whole, meaning caring for the patient and their significant others by addressing their physical, emotional, and spiritual well-being. My experience at this hospital emphasized the importance of this philosophy, and this is an important lesson for all health-care workers. *Health-care workers must remember that patients and families need answers, communication, and empathy.* All have a story, and we need to respect that story. Hospital administrators need to set policies such as visiting rules with the patient and their family's welfare as the guidepost, not what is convenient for the hospital. Unless, of course, those policies are mandated by regulatory bodies, which no one can get around. However, that is the next lesson. *As caregivers, we need to be demanding to get the answers and care that we need. Sometimes, you just can't be nice.*

Which brings me to my amusing footnote to this part of the story. Lorena and I went to our family physician the next week for follow-up. He was pleased with her physical appearance, and we discussed plans for therapy. I would like to say that the stupid EEG was negative so we spent that whole last day in the hospital for nothing. I would also like to say that we got a diagnosis, but we didn't.

Lastly, just before I left the office, the good doctor started to chuckle. He related that he had gotten a follow-up call to Lorena's admission. The specialist shared all that had happened in the hospital, along with the fact I was a real witch and my poor elderly husband just stood there and let me be that way. I found this to be hysterical. Lorena had been in the hospital for a whole week, and they didn't even know what her father looked like and thought my dad was him!

The Holy Grail:
The Pursuit for Normal

Neverland was the first stop on the road to the holy grail, which is the pursuit of normal. And to become normal, I felt we needed to first get a diagnosis. Over the course of the first two years of Lorena's life, we saw several specialists. I learned quickly that although they couldn't give us a diagnosis, they were good at giving prognoses. And each prognosis usually started with never.

We went to see the neurologist for follow up a month after Lorena's discharge from the pediatric hospital. I had learned by now that in this teaching facility you never got to see the specialist without seeing one of his posse of interns.

I learned that this posse's main job was to gather information, which had a two-fold purpose. Purpose one: the intern learned to take a history; purpose two: the intern funneled the data to the busy specialist. Being a past nursing student, I knew the importance of learning to take a patient's history, but as a mother, I was irritated by the constant questioning and answering of the same questions. So, I started to keep a calendar. I would jot important details down on the date they occurred. For instance, Lorena sat up in the tripod stance at age eleven months. Again, this is when it was handy that I was a nurse because I knew the lingo and milestones the specialists were looking for, so I had a cheat sheet format to my calendars. I would then hand the calendar to whoever was asking the questions. The calendar saved me from all those "when" questions: "When did she first smile/sit up/crawl?" The calendar also was more accurate than my memory. Stress and fatigue do not promote the ability to play "remember when," and I'll bet if you look back in those old charts, there was a different answer to "when did she smile" at every doctor's visit. This way I kept answers straight and got out of the Twenty Questions game each visit.

After the intern left, we would then be held hostage in the room for endless hours. Mike and I would take turns sitting in the one cement-seat chair, pacing the four-foot room, entertaining Lorena and peering into the hallway, looking for signs of other life forms. Eventually the neurologist came into the room, didn't make eye contact, and read all the notes the intern had written. He repeated some of the questions. He spent a few minutes looking at Lorena. He asked about her progress in therapy. He reviewed her test results from the hospital, which had all been negative, and then dismissed us with, "Okay, we'll see you in three months."

I, of course, was not satisfied. "Wait a minute, what do you think is going on?" He answered that he did not have a diagnosis but gave us his prognosis.

"Well, she will probably never have a pincer grasp, be able to crawl, and never talk." I was stunned. He then wrote something on her visit paper and said, "Now, don't look at this. It is just something so the insurance company will pay for the visit." So, like a good mother, I opened up that paper and looked right at the diagnosis: cerebral palsy.

The words screamed through my brain. I don't know how many of you have ever had a diagnosis attached to you—cancer, heart attack, stroke—but your mind instantly conjures up the worst scenario. I immediately visualized every child I had seen on my pediatric rotation in a wheelchair, with a feeding tube. While that image was burning into my brain, the neurologist looked at me and said, "I told you not to look at that." I began to tremble in anger, and I am really good at being mad.

I looked right at him. "Did you really think I wasn't going to look? Do you think that is what is wrong?"

He sighed, and I could tell by his face that he thought if I had just listened to him we wouldn't have to discuss this. "No, I told you it is just for the insurance company."

Trembling, I replied, "I don't know how you can give me a prognosis when you don't even have a diagnosis." I was outraged. How dare he take away all of our hope! I gathered up Lorena, and Mike and I went out of the office. I refused to make a return appointment. Sobbing, I clutched Lorena all the way out to the car.

Mike, the nonmedical father, tried to comfort me, although he wasn't really sure what had just happened. I tend to forget that not everyone went to nursing school. All Mike knew was that he had taken a day off work, sat in an office for hours, watched me again get irate at a doctor, heard a foreign diagnosis, and then got really scared when I started to sob. He got in the car and said, "What is cerebral palsy?" I started to sob harder and could barely answer. I also went into protective mode. I just couldn't burn the image that was in my brain into his. I carefully explained what cerebral palsy was and gave him the mildest picture I could paint realistically.

I am grateful to the neurologist for one recommendation, though. He was the one who referred us to Early Intervention. Early Intervention is a federal program that identifies children who either have a potential for developmental delay or have a developmental delay. These programs are for children and their families from birth to school age. The premise is that the younger the child, the easier to enhance the child's abilities. The program's goals and services are admirable. They were a lifesaver for us. However, like all federal programs, the red tape to get into the program was a major hassle.

First, the county health department nurse had to come to our home and assess Lorena and us. Of course, I ran around like a maniac, making sure the house was immaculate. I was afraid the dust bunnies and clutter of our lives would somehow demonstrate how inadequate I was as a mother to care for this child. The nurse, however, was wonderful. She sat on the floor and played with Lorena while I completed the million-question assessment she brought.

The questions took me by surprise, even though they probably shouldn't have. The one that particularly stuck in my mind was, "Do you spank your child?" I looked at Lorena. She was nine months old and couldn't feed herself or sit up. Her left arm was weaker than the right, so at times she became frustrated because she couldn't hold toys in her left hand and transfer them to her right. Who in their right mind would spank a child with these difficulties? And for what? I started to tremble and became slightly nauseated, as I realized that this nurse actually had to assess and make sure I wasn't abusing my child. I remember thinking, *So, because she is delayed, I am suspect for abuse? Or does the stress of the delay make parents more likely to abuse?* It broke my heart. My emotions were pretty close to the surface during this time, I struggled through the rest of the visit, trying not to cry. I was afraid to break down; to present myself as not in control or coping. Who knew how that would appear? We made it to the end, though, with me tear free, questions answered, and the nurse appearing pleased with her findings. She told me that we would be contacted shortly to get Lorena enrolled in the program.

Early Intervention can be home based, hospital based, or school based. Our county had a school-based program Lorena was eligible for. We waited for the phone call. And waited. And waited.

I must explain at this point that I have the patience of a gnat. I have almost never heard the microwave timer ding because I usually stop it before it is done. After two weeks, I was on the horn with the program director, checking on our progress. "It takes time; we have to get the paperwork in place." Another two weeks, and another phone call; the director assured me that Lorena would be starting soon. I kept hearing the echoes of those "nevers" from the doctor in my head. I was sure every day that passed cemented those "nevers" into my daughter's future. Another two weeks—my fears were peaking, my patience was gone, and I heard, "Well, I am the only one who does this, and it takes time." By now you understand I "find my mad" really quickly. Anger reared its ugly head. I asked her exactly how long this was going to take, how my daughter was supposed to progress without help, and what I was supposed to do in the meantime. She gave me a date she hoped to have it done by. When all was said and done, Lorena entered the program three months after her initial assessment, a few weeks before her first birthday.

I understand paperwork has to be done. I understand rules have to be followed. I understand sometimes you are the only person doing a job and it takes time. I understand I don't have the only child on earth who needs help. I understood all of that in my head. My mother's heart did not understand any of it. All I wanted was my child to be helped and now! Right now! And this was one of the most important lessons of all: *You are your best advocate.*

There are people out there who are paid to help you: doctors, social workers, and teachers. There are also people in your life who want to help, but you are the only one living your experience. No matter how much they all want to help, this is not their life; they have other things on their plates besides you. This is when you learn that it is all about you and you need to get selfish with your demands. And let's face it, we have all seen the news and commercials telling us that the incidents of autism are increasing. In my area—and I am sure this is pretty typical—while the number of diagnoses is increasing, I have not seen the number of therapists, specialists, and treatment programs keeping up with the increase.

There is a reason that old saying "the squeaky wheel gets the oil" is true. Throughout my health-care career and throughout this experience, I have seen many patients not get exactly what they need because they simply give up when faced with all the obstacles. When you or someone in your family is facing a crisis, you face a multitude of emotions. And coating all those emotions is fatigue, both emotionally and physically. It is daunting to keep plugging away when your body and mind are so tired and no one is taking care of you and yours. Unfortunately, if you don't keep at it, the situation will stay the same.

Finally, Lorena and I were heading out of Neverland. I didn't think the therapists would provide a diagnosis, but I did think they were the ticket to the Land of Normal. I was sure they would fix whatever development delays Lorena had and we would get back on track with our normal lives. What I didn't know was that we actually had gotten out of Neverland and were on the looping Highway of Specialists.

The therapists that day outlined a therapy strategy based on Lorena's delays. However, they couldn't answer those burning questions of why she had the delays. I felt at this point that Lorena's delays were related to her illness, but I wanted to be sure that was true.

We still saw our family physician frequently. He also hypothesized that it was probably related to her illness but couldn't be 100 percent sure. We discussed seeing another specialist. The saying is that three is the charm, and we hoped this would be true of our third specialist. But as usual, we encountered obstacles. First, we didn't know what kind of specialist she needed to see. She had delays in gross motor function (the big muscle groups that accomplish tasks such as walking), fine motor function (the control that helps you accomplish the tasks of daily living, such as picking up a spoon), and speech delays. We could have started with a pediatrician, but after dealing with the pediatrician who gave us the "floppy" diagnosis, I wasn't too keen on pursuing that. I knew that stereotyping was dangerous, but I just couldn't get past that experience.

How do you begin, then? I started with what I had at hand. Lorena was born in 1991, so research was a completely different arena at this time. I had her list of symptoms and started by looking at pediatric books from my own and the hospital's medical library. Sounds ridiculous in today's world, where all I need to do is Google some symptoms. It was a time-consuming process, and I would not get very far very fast.

I was still working full time, taking care of two kids, and being a wife and a homemaker. And we were taking Lorena to therapy four times a week for three-hour visits. Somewhere in all that, I tried to sleep a little. I also read any newspaper article or journal I could find.

I actually selected the next specialist due to a TV program. One night I was flipping through the channels and heard the words "development delay." PBS was highlighting a physician in Toledo who specialized in development delays. I was so excited. I was sure I had hit pay dirt. I didn't realize at that time that the Highway of Specialists is paved with speed bumps.

Speed bump one is the insurance company. Actually, today, speed bump number one is even having insurance. In a 2009 article, Trapp estimates that more than 46 million Americans are uninsured, and of that number, 7.3 million are children (American Medical News)[1]. Mike and I found that specialists' fees begin in the hundreds per visit and can range up into the thousands. A general practitioner or pediatrician's visit ranges in our area from sixty-five dollars to over one hundred dollars per visit. The office fee is not the only cost, either. Many times you have to take off work, which can mean lost wages. I am so grateful that we both have insurance and have not had to deal with that, because I guess that is not just a speed bump, but a dead-end road in many cases.

I expressed earlier my fears in regard to time passing and the effect it would have on Lorena. I cannot imagine what it would feel like to not have the hope of being able to pursue the possibilities for help. As a parent, that horrifies me.

Even if you have insurance, though, all insurance and coverage is different. At that time, we just needed to get a referral from our family physician. I feel that we are lucky because we had a relationship with our family physician and he knew me as a nurse, which I think helped. A visit to him, and we were referred. Many times, it is not that simple. Today, you might be denied because the specialist is not in the network, which results in either a denied visit or a higher co-pay. You might be denied based on the type of specialist or for any other reason. I learned two important lessons during the process of making specialist appointments: *You should always get the denial in writing* and *you can appeal denials.*

These lessons carried over not only for making appointments with specialists, but in getting treatments or therapies approved. The physician would order a treatment, therapy, or medication. I would call to see if it was covered. The insurance company representative would tell me it was not covered. I have never understood exactly how insurances decide what is covered and what is not. For instance, when Lorena needed speech therapy, the insurance company denied. They did not cover speech therapy when it was needed for development delays. They did not cover speech therapy if you were born with a hearing deficit. I asked when speech therapy was covered. They paid for speech therapy for children who had frequent ear infections and had tubes in their ears. Voila! Lorena had tubes in her ears due to frequent infections. I made sure that was listed as the reason for her speech therapy, and it was covered. It was true, and since we didn't have a diagnosis, we couldn't say why she wasn't talking; maybe it was the infections and tubes. This is one of the few times during this early period that I was actually glad Lorena's disability did not have an official diagnosis yet. I started to learn that a diagnosis might actually work against you from an insurance standpoint.

This experience led me to a mental picture of the insurance company's decision-making process. I visualized a bunch of executives sitting around a table, eating donuts, drinking coffee, and puffing cigars, debating how to eke the most profit out of the premiums we all pay. The conversation would go like this.

"So, next up is speech therapy."

"Speech therapy, you mean for like deaf kids or kids who are handicapped? We can't do that; they will need it forever. Do you know what that will cost?"

"Yeah, but we can't just not give kids speech therapy; that would be mean. I know, let's only give it to kids with ear infections and tubes. They won't need it long, and we will look like we care. I mean, more kids have infections than are born without hearing, so we at least cover some."

Executives grin and grunt in approval. A win-win for everybody, right? I know that is insulting, but in my head, that is how I picture it. I guess that is better than actually picturing them throwing darts at a board with diagnosis to see what they will cover. And with that picture in mind, autism is one of the diagnoses historically not covered by private insurance companies. According to Autism Speaks, an organization dedicated to autism advocacy, most private insurance companies have clauses that specifically exclude coverage of autism-related therapies[2].

Disregarding this image in my head, I would ask how to get it covered. The answer is that the physician needs to write a letter. This can become another speed bump, because these letters can be delayed getting out of the busy doctor's office. You are important, but so are the hundred or even thousands of other patients in the practice. Remember, I am not a patient person. My impatience spurred me to write the letters myself.

I developed a simple format. I would start the letter by introducing Lorena and the requested service. Then, since I was a nurse, I knew I needed to provide evidence to support the need for the service. I found two Web sites to be the most helpful: the National Institute of Health (NIH) (http://www.nih.gov) and the Center for Disease Control (CDC) (http://www.cdc.gov/). These two organizations are both government agencies, and they both have disease and symptom research and articles. I like these because I can trust the data. They also have links to the major support groups for many diseases, which is another excellent resource for evidence. Lastly, if neither of these has the disease or symptoms you need, I would start with the National Organization of Rare Diseases, or NORD (http://www.rarediseases. org). This organization has information as advertised, those diseases that are rare or not publicly known. (I cite this information just like I am writing an English research paper.)

Another lesson: *keep a copy of the letter you wrote for future reference and the approval/denial letter from the insurance company.* Sometimes, even though they have approved the procedure when the claim is submitted, it will be denied. Then you have to call the insurance company and say, "Hey,

I've got the letter in my hand that says it is approved." They will look it up on their computer, find the letter, and then send the claim to be reprocessed. Sometimes this step is like shampooing your hair. You might have to call, explain, and repeat a few times before the claim is settled.

Insurance is probably the most frustrating and heart-breaking speed bump. It is also the most time consuming. Again, it is horrifying when you know that your child needs a service and you cannot provide the service. In addition, you are exhausted from dealing with everything, and now you have to fight this battle. The phone calls, research, return phone calls, delays waiting for return phone calls, and the care of your child, plus trying to work and maintain a home absolutely drain you. Nothing seems to happen quickly or fall into your lap, so this zaps a great deal of the little energy you have. And in the back of your mind, you see all those milestones your child will never reach if they don't start getting help soon. So guilt also layers on the rest of your turmoil.

If you are lucky and you get over the insurance speed bump, the next step is making the appointment to see the specialist. I was used to calling a family physician's office and at most, waiting a few days to see the doctor. I was floored to learn that the earliest appointment we could get with the specialist was several months away. I know that there are a limited number of specialists for each specialty, but again, the idea of those "nevers" becoming cemented in Lorena's life haunted me. I was glad that at least before we saw the doctor, Lorena was getting therapy through Early Intervention and privately. Even if we didn't have the diagnosis, at least the symptoms were being treated. In the vague world of development delays, the diagnosis can take years. If you wait those years to treat the delays, they will become those "nevers." At least if your child is having delays in speech and gets some type of speech therapy, you more than likely will see some progress.

As with Early Intervention, I waited impatiently for this appointment. I was anxious and fearful, while at the same time hopeful. I also had researched quite a bit by this time. I was convinced that Lorena was autistic. Autism Speaks defines autism as a complex neurobiological disorder that typically lasts throughout a person's lifetime. It is part of a group of disorders known as autism spectrum disorders (ASD). Autism impairs a person's ability to communicate with and relate to others. It is also associated with rigid routines and repetitive behaviors, such as obsessively arranging objects or following very specific routines. Symptoms can range from very mild to quite severe[3].

At fourteen months, Lorena's language skills were almost nonexistent. There weren't any "mamas" or "dadas," much less words. She did make noises, especially this awful, keening scream when she was upset. I noticed that she did not look at anyone directly in the eyes. She tended to look at people out of the corner of her eyes. I think the best way to describe her personality at this point was flat. She hardly ever smiled, giggled, or interacted with us. I did recognize that she seemed to understand everything I said to her. I could tell by the way she responded, and she would look at me when I called her name. I also noted that she seemed to have trouble with touching items.

Lorena started to crawl at around eighteen months. I would watch as she slowly moved from room to room. She would stop at the doorway at each room and feel the floor of the next room. Depending on the texture of the floor or carpet, she would not crawl into certain rooms. She would not touch stuffed animals. I observed that you could hold her wrist, but if you tried to hold her hand, she would curl her fingers and pull away. I did not notice repetitive behaviors at this time, but she was delayed physically by several months and required assistance to accomplish almost everything. I don't think she had enough independence yet to determine if she was displaying this symptom. In addition, she did not do well with change at all. A change in routine would result in a massive meltdown.

The day of the appointment finally arrived; the all-important appointment that I was sure was finally going to confirm a diagnosis for us. Lorena was fourteen months old without reaching many of those milestones the average baby had aced at this age. We drove the hour to the clinic. This was another speed bump, as far as I was concerned. Every specialist we ever consulted was at least one hour away, so you knew your whole day was gone with each appointment: two hours to drive back and forth, at least fifteen minutes for paperwork, anywhere from fifteen minutes to one hour in the waiting room, and up to another thirty minutes cooling your heels in the exam room. Then ten to fifteen minutes with a nurse and one of the posse of interns or residents. It always amazed me that we never actually had contact with the specialist more than twenty minutes out of all that time.

This particular specialist also had a social worker meet with us to make sure we were getting the services we needed. This would have been a more appreciated gesture if the first question out of the social worker's mouth had not been, "Was she sexually abused?" I just remembered my sick horror that this was her introductory question. For some reason, she also seemed to reside in Neverland and kept repeating the first specialist's litany of "nevers." I got the distinct impression that she thought I was in denial and felt it was her duty to shake me out of it. I am not saying that I wasn't in some form of denial, but the flip side of denial is hope. And hope makes you push forward and keep fighting. I certainly was not willing at this point to give up on a fourteen-month-old. I quickly realized this social worker and I were not going to be buddies.

Finally we were in the room with the specialist. She examined Lorena and questioned us carefully. I felt comfortable with her. She communicated well, did not go to Neverland, and seemed committed to helping us find answers. She suggested we start with genetic testing. I ventured forth with my hypothesis. "Do you think she could be autistic?" She asked me to say Lorena's name. I did; Lorena looked me straight in the eye in response. The doctor then told me she couldn't be autistic because there were ten criteria, and Lorena only met three of them. Lorena looked when I called her name, was demonstrating repetitive behavior, and was not verbal. I don't know what the remainder of the ten were, but I do know that today I don't think a specialist would say that. The problem then and the comfort now is that sixteen years ago, autism was not as recognized or researched as it is today. Today, autism is recognized as a spectrum disorder. This means that while some people with autism display all of the characteristics to a great degree, some have minimal symptoms, which explains why Lorena displayed three out of the ten.

I did like this specialist, though, and her approach. She had a game plan in regard to tests and services instead of handing me a prognosis without a diagnosis. So off Mike, Lorena, and

I went to the lab to have blood drawn for genetic testing. I found this to be especially scary. First, poor Lorena had spent her entire life since she was four months old being poked and prodded. She emitted a piercing shriek while the blood was drawn. Her father is not exactly made of sterner stuff when it comes to blood draws. He generally passes out; that's right, this six-foot-two-inch man goes down like a fallen tree at the sight of a needle. But we managed to get all three of us through the blood draw. We also met briefly with the geneticist. Again, we began the waiting game; genetic testing results took a minimum of six to eight weeks to return.

I had asked the specialist if I could call and get the results. She was hesitant to do this. They really preferred to give them face-to-face. I played the nurse trump card. I would be okay. I was sure I could handle the results over the phone, and I didn't want to spend another day traveling just to get test results. I called the day they told me the results would be back.

I will never forget that phone call. I was standing looking out our living room window at a bright, sunny afternoon. She relayed to me that Lorena's test results showed positive for a syndrome called Fragile X. It also showed that Mike and I were both carriers. While I won't say I was happy, I was relieved to finally have an answer. My relief was short-lived when I asked her if this was a genetic disorder like Down syndrome, where it is a chromosomal anomaly present in that person, or one like cystic fibrosis, which is a disorder passed genetically from the parents. Her words shattered my world: it was inherited. Mickey would have to be tested too.

I had gained a diagnosis for my daughter. I also had just lost hope for my future. If Mickey was a carrier, what did that mean for his life, his children? I don't remember the rest of the phone call. I do remember agreeing to take Mickey to get his blood drawn for testing.

I sobbed the rest of the day. As the news sank in, the realization came that this diagnosis affected my whole family. If we were carriers, who else in the family was? Immediately, I began to look for information. Remember, no Google at the time. I started by calling the Early Intervention coordinator. She was the one who told me about National Organization of Rare Diseases (NORD). I contacted them, and they were able to send me information.

The information confused me, though. The National Fragile X Foundation defines Fragile X as a family of genetic conditions which can impact individuals and families in various ways. These genetic conditions are related in that they are all caused by gene changes in the same gene, called the FMR1 gene. The foundation further relates that it is the most common cause of inherited mental impairment. This impairment can range from learning disabilities to more severe cognitive or intellectual disabilities (sometimes referred to as mental retardation). It is the most common known cause of autism or autistic-like behaviors. Symptoms can also include characteristic physical and behavioral features and delays in speech and language development.[4]

The definition and facts seemed to relate to what I was seeing in Lorena. What confused me, though, was the information in one pamphlet that discussed how the disorder showed in generations of families. One article particularly discussed how many families had previous generations of relatives that had been labeled retarded or autistic but due to the lack of genetic testing had never been correctly diagnosed as Fragile X. I looked through our family trees, and this simply did not fit. I theorized this must be a new mutation. Was that possible? I finally found some sources that suggested that possibility. I also was struck by the fact that Mickey was normal. Since Fragile X is a problem with a chromosome on the X gene, and males only have one X gene, the disorder is more pronounced in them. Females have two X chromosomes, so the one X covers for the malformation in the other one, which makes the symptoms milder. I understood from the explanations that there was a one in four chance that Mickey would be born without the gene, which made me hopeful he was not a carrier. I also questioned how Mike could just be a carrier.

This exploration was rough on my extended family. I can't begin to explain all the emotions this diagnosis brings to a family. Some members panicked, wanting their children to be tested immediately. Mike had some young nieces and nephews who were just beginning to date, and the parents questioned what this meant to them. Some family members were angry. It couldn't be true; no one in the family had it. I asked my parents to be tested, and they resisted. What did it matter? But it mattered to me because if they had it, then we needed to let that side of the family know. Genetic testing at this time, though, was seen as radical, so they just didn't buy into it. Many family members took a wait-and-see attitude. I think before this diagnosis, Lorena's problems concerned them, but they didn't own them. This diagnosis suddenly gave them some ownership and it was not a welcome event. Suddenly, our family's entire medical history had changed.

While I was busy researching all of this, I heard of another family in Early Intervention whose daughter was diagnosed with Fragile X. In addition, both parents had also been told they were carriers. The Early Intervention coordinator asked the family for permission for me to contact them. I about fell off my chair when I heard the name. The mother was one of my fellow nursing students from my diploma-nursing program. In addition, she had taken her daughter to the same specialist we had seen to get the Fragile X diagnosis. Small, small world. We began to call, tell our stories, and support each other. Her daughter also had multiple physical problems that required additional care and surgery. Coincidentally, she had the same questions in regards to Fragile X that I had.

Her daughter went in for surgery, and I called after she got home to see how everyone was doing. She told me that she had been debating calling me because she had some news and wasn't sure how to tell me. Her daughter had gone to a large university hospital for her surgery. One of the specialists at that facility told her that he just didn't believe her daughter had Fragile X. They redid the genetic test, and the results came back completely different. She contacted the specialist we had both seen, and this specialist admitted that they had noticed a problem with the testing and knew her results were wrong. Let me repeat that: they knew her results were wrong but had not contacted her. The mother asked the specialists about other people tested there, and the specialist waffled. I was livid. What did that mean for us? Had they been wrong?

Unfortunately, this phone call took place on a Friday evening, so I had to wait until Monday morning. I chose not to tell my husband over the weekend. We had been on such a roller coaster; how could I put him through another ride? I chose to worry alone. First thing Monday morning, I called the specialist.

I was not nice on the phone—I was very demanding— and I am sure the words *malpractice* and *lawsuit* came into my vocabulary. When I got her on the phone, the specialist admitted that our results were also not correct. They had redone them, and Lorena did not have Fragile X; Mike and I were not carriers. I exploded. I remember yelling, "And when were you going to tell us this?" She admitted that the geneticists and she had been consulting and trying to decide the best way to notify us. The best way to notify us? How about a phone call saying, "Oops, screwed up, you're all negative." As far as I was concerned, they were just trying to cover themselves. She asked if we would come see her and the geneticist. I flatly refused.

I immediately started the family phone chain. You can imagine my family's reaction. Now all their worries and concerns were put to rest, but they had spent at least six months thinking the family had a time bomb in their chromosomes. It had an effect on everyone. I loudly vented to anyone who would listen about this disaster. My boss at that time asked what I would like to see happen. That got me thinking. I called the specialist back. I told her my list of demands. I wanted the tests repeated at an outside lab at the specialist's cost, the original cost reimbursed to the insurance company, and a letter of apology from the geneticist. I also wanted to know how many families had gotten these wrong results. Now she knew I knew of at least two, so that was the answer I got: two. I still don't believe it, and I still wonder if there are families out there who never got the correct results.

All my demands were satisfied, including the letter, but it wasn't an apology. I figured it wouldn't be because of liability reasons; they were not going to admit wrongdoing. Remember, the geneticist and specialist wanted to meet with us again. So the letter indicated that I was noncompliant and did not return for follow-up, so they couldn't update the results. I was too exhausted and overwrought to deal with that at this point. I was just relieved when the second set of test results from the next facility came back negative.

Whenever people hear this part of our story, they ask why we didn't sue. I tried actually. Mike and I discussed doing just that. I worried first about all those other families I was questioning weren't told the truth. So I began by calling reporters. It must have gotten back to the facility, because I got a phone call from the geneticist's office telling me I could be in trouble for slander. I was not as strong or sure then as I am today, so I hushed up. Today, I know how to state things, and I would have just stuck to the facts and let the paper do their job. I also did call attorneys, but they told me that it was hard to win a genetic case. I finally decided it just was not worth my energy.

I have seen the toll that lawsuits take on families. First, the suits don't usually resolve quickly. Secondly, they take up valuable resources: time, money, and energy that I just couldn't spare. Thirdly, when you are actively pursuing a lawsuit, you can't move on past what has hurt you. You continuously live it until the lawsuit is complete. And if it isn't concluded justly in your mind, you might never resolve the hurt. I just didn't have enough resources to pursue that with everything else in my life. The focus needed to be my family, and now we were back to square one, trying to find a diagnosis for Lorena. With those factors in mind, I still feel that Mike and I made the right decision for us.

My lesson was that *you need to trust your gut.* My gut kept telling me that this diagnosis was not the answer. I just felt that there were too many questions that did not have logical answers. As a parent you need to listen to your gut and pursue the right answers until it rings true with you.

The more painful lesson is not one I wish on anyone else. I lost my trust in the specialists. I just could not bring myself to continue to pursue a diagnosis with this route. We continued to see our family physician, I continued to research options, and Lorena continued to get therapy, but I did not seek another specialist's opinion for a few years. By the time the Fragile X fiasco was done, Lorena was almost three years of age. Most of those "nevers" were not coming true. She was walking, could feed herself, had a pincer grasp. However, there still was not any verbal speech. I also had begun to notice those repetitive behaviors that I felt indicated autism. She would spend hours looking at the same page in books and magazines, making a toy repeat a motion or a sound. She also still had difficulty with any change in routine, which would result in a massive meltdown.

Shortly after Lorena's fifth birthday, I was discussing a new therapy with our family physician and I asked him, "Do you think Lorena is autistic?"

He nodded. "I think so." So anticlimactic. No bells, no whistles, just finally the diagnosis I had suspected much earlier.

I sit here today, knowing we never did obtain the holy grail of normal that we set out pursuing. However, I do know that we have found our own normal. It is not the future I envisioned, but it is one where Lorena is pushed to achieve her potential and one where her family is okay with her and what we have become. I think many families fall short in the "normal" category. I learned that *each family has its own normal, and that is the ability to function in whatever set of circumstances they have been given.*

Communication 101

Lorena is nonverbal. The first specialist predicted in his litany of "nevers" that she would never talk. I was so angry with him because I felt he couldn't give us a diagnosis. I also was devastated. How would I ever know what she needed, wanted, or thought? I also admit that in my mind, speech meant intelligence, so did that mean she was mentally retarded? Friends often tease me that I live way too much in my head. I am a thinker, a ponderer, and I so wanted to share that ability with my daughter. The idea that I wouldn't was almost more than I could take. I fantasized that this specialist was wrong. I was going to teach Lorena to speak.

That fantasy never came true. Communication problems are one of the cardinal symptoms of autism. The National Institute on Deafness and Other Communication Disorders (NIDCD) states, "The communication problems of autism vary, depending upon the intellectual and social development of the individual. Some may be unable to speak, whereas others may have rich vocabularies and are able to talk about topics of interest in great depth. Despite this variation, the majority of autistic individuals have little or no problem with pronunciation. Most have difficulty effectively using language. Many also have problems with word and sentence meaning, intonation, and rhythm."[5]

We struggled with Lorena's communication issues. I often felt that we were in Communication 101 with no syllabus and Lorena was the professor. All we knew was that Lorena was not developing speech at all. No cooing, no mamas, no dadas, and no imitating animal sounds. She had developed one sure-fire communication method, though. She would begin to cry and escalate to a keening shrill scream if we didn't figure out quickly what she needed. That sound traveled right down your spine, and believe me, it made you quick to figure out what she needed. At this point in Lorena's development, she didn't gesture either. I know this sounds bizarre, but she just couldn't figure out how to point to what she wanted. So we literally had to teach her how to lift up her arm and point a finger at what she wanted. When she finally got that concept, it was a momentous event at our house.

Her speech therapists tried to help us get past this point-and-scream method. We knew that all Lorena's physical exams, MRIs, and CTs did not show any reason that she could not talk. Our working hypothesis without a diagnosis was that we were rewarding her point and scream, and we needed to teach her to ask for items. We began by trying to get her to make sounds for certain items.

The one I particularly remember is milk. She would crawl into the kitchen and begin that nerve-shattering keen. I would figure, *Okay, kitchen, she must be hungry or thirsty*. I would say, "Milk?" I would pour the milk while this keening would start to escalate, and then sit her on the counter.

I would hold the cup up and try to get her to at least make the "m" sound. By now she would be bouncing her whole body and her screaming had reached crystal-shattering decibels. I gave her the milk. I just couldn't stand it. My gut just told me this wasn't going to work. However, this is a widely accepted practice called Verbal Behavior Intervention, and many autism resources recognize it as an appropriate and effective therapy.

Was I right to just give her the milk with that knowledge? I don't know. I think you should try anything, but if you don't get results over a period of time, you need to decide if it is the right tool for you. We tried this process over and over, and not just with milk. We still try to get her to imitate sounds. Rarely, she will imitate noises. She does pronounce one word clearly and appropriately: no.

She seemed to learn how to say "no" all on her own, like any typical toddler who hears the phrase repeatedly. She also uses it very appropriately and emphatically. I think this is representative of the mysteries of an autistic brain. How could she perfectly say and use that one word but not others? This mystery deepens when she suddenly will say another word clearly. For instance, Lorena loves to look at babies. She will become excited, pointing and signing when a baby is in view. A few times when she signed, Lorena said "aby." The "b" was not clear, but the meaning was. That is why Mike and I continue to encourage her to make sounds and verbalizations. I am not convinced that Lorena will always be non-verbal. Wishful thinking? False hope? Maybe. But that hope helps us keep to continue on our journey to hearing Lorena's voice.

Pictures and storyboards were the next step in our communication journey. The speech therapists used pictures to teach Lorena vocabulary. The pictures don't have to be fancy either. Magazines, books, and family photos all work. Most parents do this automatically with their children anyway. You just take the pictures and ask, "Where is the bird?" The child points at the bird. Except with autism, the child pointing at the bird sometimes takes days, weeks, months. And even if they do finally point at the bird, they might not do it again for days, weeks, months. Does this mean they don't know what a bird is? I am not sure. I think language, as we who are typical think of language, is a slippery concept for them and at times some of the vocabulary they have learned does come and go. I also think that people with autism have sensory issues, which distract them and make them unable to focus on what a bird is that day. I do know that pictures have been a godsend for us. Gesturing was a huge step for her, but being able to pick up a picture and show us what she wanted was a tremendous leap too.

The use of pictures also helps overcome another obstacle of autism. People with autism have difficulty with change or transition from one activity to another. They have an intense need for order and organization. This is an obstacle because in a typical life or classroom, the day doesn't always progress the same way each day. The picture schedule is a tool to help this transition. They are also pretty inexpensive and simple to make. The ones I have seen at school are usually on a bulletin board. There are pictures of activities, and they are lined up on the board in the order they will occur that day. The pictures can be taped or Velcroed to the board. At one school, they actually had a wooden board with teacup hooks to hang the pictures. I accomplished this at home by purchasing a small, inexpensive corkboard. I bought Velcro circles at the store. I then took pictures of various activities. I would Velcro Lorena's schedule to the board for the day, starting with getting out of bed, getting dressed, eating breakfast, and so on.

This was not an overnight fix. They still use the picture schedule at school. I would say it has taken from her entrance into the school system at age three until she reached the age of sixteen to state the schedule was successful in helping her deal with transitions. In fact, her Individual Education Plan (IEP) still has a goal every year that Lorena will learn how to transition from activity to activity smoothly. But I do know that these transitions are happening more smoothly every year.

What do I mean by smoother? It used to be that each time Lorena had to switch from one activity to another she would have a major meltdown. Today, we are to the point where she might protest by yelling a little, but the outburst stops in a few moments. In fact, at home we don't use the picture schedule anymore and are able to verbally direct her through the day.

Sign language is another tool we tried. The Early Intervention therapist started using American Sign Language with Lorena first. The speech therapist at the rehabilitation hospital did not. I had always thought that all speech therapists were proficient in sign language. I don't know why I thought this, but in my logical little brain I just assumed if you were going to be working with patients, including deaf patients, that you would know sign language. I have found that while most speech therapists have some knowledge of sign language, proficiency takes additional education. In addition, even if your speech therapist is proficient, your child's teacher probably is not. And somehow, you have to teach yourself.

I looked for classes in our area. They required a huge time commitment and cost because most of them were through community colleges. Then, after you learn it, you have to teach everyone else—friends and family—the signs too, which doesn't work for that cousin you only see twice a year.

My second assumption was that sign language is sign language. Wrong. The NIDCD relates that "no one form of sign language is universal. For example, British Sign Language (BSL) differs notably from ASL. Different sign languages are used in different countries or regions." [6]

So now we had a tool that could be useful but had a few pitfalls. I did find that most of the teachers had a small vocabulary of basic signs—potty, more, eat, drink, and thank you. Lorena picked up a few signs quickly, but she only used them if we prompted her and did the sign with her. She tended to use "more" for everything, and we let her get away with that for a while. She also tweaked the signs. She would do them just a little bit differently, which we understood, but someone who knew the right signs might not.

We found that the best tool is the communication board. The communication board is an electronic device. You slide a group of pictures (which I am going to call a sheet because I print them on a legal-length sheet of paper and laminate them) on to the front of the device. The pictures are created a couple of different ways. You can cut pictures out and paste them to a sheet. You also can buy software, which has a library of pictures. We bought the software. The library is huge, with thousands of pictures, from colors to holidays to sex. Mike and I had to giggle over the sex pictures for a bit when we first started learning how to use the software. The software is not cheap, though, and because of copyright laws, it can only be loaded on one computer. However, if you want to share the cost with others, load it on one computer and then create and print from that one computer; that is your business. The sheets are best laminated because when you slide them in or out, the pictures catch and can pull off. We bought a small laminator for about $75 at a local office supply store.

The device uses a push screen. You can record your voice to name objects, ask questions, voice requests, etc. The simplest of these that I have seen has four slots. Hypothetically, if I were going to use that, I could program a sheet with a picture of a person nodding their head "yes," a picture of a person shaking their head "no," a picture of a toilet, and a combined picture with the signs for eat and drink. I could then record me saying, "Yes," "No," "I have to go to the bathroom," and "I want to eat or drink." The more complex (in other words, expensive) boards have a level switch, and each level can have up to forty-eight phrases. We purchased a board somewhere in the middle price range. We were lucky enough to get this board paid for by the insurance company. The cost was $600. This tool is useful because it "speaks" for Lorena, so everyone can understand what she is "saying." I am sure you have been adding it up in your head, though, and figured out this is not a cheap option.

It has drawbacks too. First, we have to slide the sheet for each level in and out. Lorena physically has not conquered that yet. This means that if she grabs the board to tell us something and the right sheet isn't showing, she can't tell us. We got around this, though, by just leaving all the sheets laying out. She grabs the right sheet and then points to what she wants. It doesn't have the voice, but at least she is getting her point across.

The bottom line, though, is that no matter how many tools we use to understand what Lorena wants or needs, I still can't find a way to hear her thoughts or feelings. I keep thinking her communication is locked in her brain and if I could just find the right key, I would be able to unlock all those thoughts.

Trying to find the key has taught me to be a better communicator. I tell people the lesson I have learned was *to not just use my ears to listen*. I listen with my eyes too. I have to with Lorena because many times her body language, gesturing, and head movements tell me what she wants. In fact, this is not an atypical behavior. Do you know that most resources on communication will tell you that if you speak to someone, they believe your body language before they believe what you are verbally telling them? Did you also know that 80 percent of the message we communicate is sent through our body language? For instance, if someone stops me and asks if I have a minute and I say yes but I don't turn my feet and body toward them, my body is saying no. I not only have learned to watch others' body language for their message but to make sure that my own body is indicating what I want them to hear.

The eyes also become important from another perspective. If someone does not meet eye contact, we tend to think the person is not listening. We also think that if someone does not make eye contact, they are not telling the truth. People with autism often do not make direct eye contact and in fact, show signs of anxiety when they do (Stewart, n.d.).[7]

Stewart also relates that "educators have been taught that it is essential to get individuals' attention before beginning instruction and to recapture attention to task when peoples' demeanors suggest that their attention is waning. To accomplish this task, teachers often first attempt to get attention by cuing 'Look at me.'"

I was taught that by Lorena's therapists and also read it in every reference I accessed for help with her language development. So from early on when I talked to Lorena and made a request, I would ask her to look at me if she wasn't. I would even pick up her chin and force eye contact when she didn't comply. This idea of eye contact as a necessity got blown apart the first time I went to hear Sondra Williams speak. Sondra Williams is an adult with high-functioning autism. Sondra expresses herself as an author; she writes books and poetry. In addition, she presents to live audiences. I have listened to her twice now and have found it to be illuminating. I feel she is able to give me Lorena's perception of her world.

Sondra related that while people with autism often look out of the corner of their eye or above or below your face, they actually are looking at you from their perspective. In fact, she stated that when we tell them to look at us or lift their face to look at us, they are now looking at whatever is above, below, or to the side of your face. I was floored by this statement. My mom and husband were at the seminar that night, and we all agreed that we would not do that anymore.

As usual, though, Lorena put her own spin on that piece of information. We went to church that weekend. It has taken years for Lorena to be able to sit through a Mass without major disruptions. She manages this by taking books to look at or her Game Boy to play. I have decided this is appropriate because I know I can listen to the TV while doing other activities, so I figure it is the same for her. She also likes to go out to eat after church. As soon as we sit in the pew, she will sign to eat and I will assure her we are going out after church. She usually is content with this. Sometimes, though, she seems to need repeated assurance that we are indeed going out to eat after church. I will answer a few times, but then I tell her that is enough and I am listening to church. If she signs again, I usually ignore her. Well, that week, when I had ignored her insistent signing a few times, she pulled my chin with her hand to make eye contact with her and signed again. I had to bite my lip not to laugh. My mother leaned over and said, "Doesn't she know you are not supposed to do that?" Obviously she had learned that if I didn't look into her eyes, I wasn't listening.

I also think I have learned to listen through my skin. What I mean is that I have learned the power of touch as a listener. I can see when Lorena is in a situation that is making her anxious or upsetting her. She begins to make harsh noises, her body tenses, she begins to swing her head or pull on me. I can help her to prevent a full-blown meltdown by rubbing her neck, squeezing her knee, or rubbing her back. That is usually enough to decrease her anxiety or stop a meltdown. I find this is helpful in the rest of my life too. I know as a nurse, today we have more technology than ever: automatic blood pressure cuffs, electronic thermometers, too many monitors to name, and bed mattresses that change the pressure points, replacing that good old back rub. These advances have all helped us to provide better care for our patients, except I still think the patients need that good old-fashioned touch. I know when I have a grieving family member and I touch their hand to convey my sympathy, I don't have to say a word.

I also recognize that not everyone likes to be touched. Different people have different tolerances, and different cultures have different rules. But by learning and following these boundaries, you demonstrate respect for their beliefs, which is another powerful component of communication. A common assumption with people with autism is that they don't like to be touched. *Like* is the wrong word. People with autism often have tactile defensiveness.

The National Fragile X Foundation describes tactile defensiveness as "a specific type of sensory defensiveness, or hyper-arousal. Tactile defensiveness means that the person overreacts to touch and may refuse or avoid touching ... Tactile defensiveness may also include increased or decreased reactions to texture."[8] It is important when interacting with someone with autism to learn what type of touch the individual tolerates. For instance, I have related that Lorena does not like her hands held. She does like the palm and back lightly rubbed, though. She does not like to hug, but she likes to lean against you and lay her head on your shoulder.

I also have learned to listen more with my heart. It amazes me today, in this world of hyper-communication, how little we are actually communicating. We live in a world where people carry communication devices that allow them to text message, e-mail, and talk; yet I think they are communicating less. I have literally seen business people at work e-mail each other when their offices are right next door to each other.

I remember thinking when e-mail and instant messaging first became popular that it was a good thing. After all, kids were revamping that old art of letter writing. I was sure this would encourage writing skills. I should have realized that kids being kids, they would find a shortcut, creating their own language to cut the workload and frustrate parents.

E-mail presents its own communication problem. E-mail is flat. When I read an e-mail, my feelings and perceptions are attached to the e-mail. If I dislike someone, the most innocent message can become sarcastic or nasty. Emoticons help this in personal correspondence, but smiley faces are not exactly professional in a business setting.

Cell phones are another communication device that I believe decreases our ability to talk to each other. It amazes me when I look around at restaurants and see couples or groups who aren't even speaking to each other but are talking or texting on cell phones. And now we have those Bluetooth earpieces that you can't even see. I can't tell you the number of times in a store or on the street I have answered someone, thinking they were talking to me. Then they look at me like I am the strange one! We are no longer really listening to anyone. We are so over bombarded with messages in so many forms that I think we have stopped hearing.

Since we are not always listening effectively and Lorena does not communicate easily, she has taught me that *it is our job to speak for those who can't.* I have always been a strongly opinionated person. I know you are surprised. I grew up in a home where my dad insisted I had a right to my opinion. This was such an empowering philosophy. It was also one of those quirks of fate that helped me to cope with this situation.

In the early days, my greatest apprehension was people's reaction to Lorena. I loved my daughter with all the fierceness of a mother bear protecting her cub. I didn't want her ostracized or misunderstood. I would walk into situations hyperaware of people's reaction to her. I quickly began to have a script for new situations. I would explain that she had developmental delays, was nonverbal but could hear and understand, and was scared of new situations. This explanation usually sufficed with adults. I would explain to younger children that your brain is like a computer or the TV and it receives messages like they do from the mouse or the remote control. In Lorena's case, the message wasn't always being received, so it couldn't send back the right instructions so she could speak. They usually caught on quickly to that explanation.

I also felt obligated to become a voice to the community. After all, I wanted her to function in this community, so I had to help it function with her. Our local Easter egg hunt was a good example. Our local Eagles Club has an annual Easter egg hunt. It is a mad house. There are literally hundreds of eggs strewn over our community center's field. The field is sectioned off into age groups. The prizes are the plastic eggs, which entitle the finder to an Easter basket filled with goodies. The hunt starts with the fire engines screaming the start. The children scramble across the field, crushing eggs, stumbling over each other, and rushing for the plastic eggs. Parents are allowed to join the mayhem if they are assisting their children under age one. The entire event lasts approximately 2.2 seconds.

Unfortunately, the first year we felt Lorena was able to participate, she was three, which meant we couldn't help her. She wasn't walking yet, and the kids in her age group were running. In addition, the fire engine's blast scared her to death, and we couldn't put her down. The next year, as Easter approached, I decided to contact the Eagles. I explained to the auxiliary president the situation and suggested that they have a handicapped section. This was someone I knew, and she was receptive to the idea. I can't tell you how much it meant to me when I read the advertisement in the paper two days later and saw within the categories a handicapped section. No trumpets, no drum roll, just the simple inclusion of another category. I was so grateful and appreciative of this act of empathy. To them I'm sure it was just the simple task of adding a category. To me it was a momentous nod to Lorena's, and other disabled children's, acceptance by the community.

When we arrived that day, the Eagles members had roped off a section of the parking lot so the children would not have to run over the lumpy field. I also noticed that they had strategically placed orange cones with eggs balanced on top so those in wheelchairs could reach the eggs. There also seemed to be a few more plastic eggs in this area than in the general categories. My reaction at that moment is one I often experience. I wanted to sit down and weep with gratitude that someone had made this effort to understand and help.

I also recognized for the first time how many families in Bellevue there were with children with disabilities. I hadn't just spoken for Lorena; I had spoken for them. We have a children's home in the area that is dedicated to providing a home to children with disabilities. The home brought kids by the vanload. When that fire truck screamed and the "normal" kids were racing madly out in the field, these kids were crawling, limping, and wheeling with glee toward the eggs. Our hunt took longer, but the outcome was the same: smiles, excitement, and Easter baskets full of goodies.

That is a small example of parent as advocate. Two mothers' advocacy efforts helped to establish a program in our area that was a godsend to us in Lorena's early school years. They approached a local hospital to develop a program to support parents and kids with autism. The program became affectionately known in our home as "autism camp." Autism camp met a few times a year for six weeks at a time. The children with autism were each assigned a buddy. This buddy was a typical older child or adult who helped them through the scheduled activities for the day. The activities varied from arts and crafts to music therapy to karate. The goal for the kids was to increase language, help tactile defensiveness, and increase social interaction. The goal for the parents was support and information exchange.

I will never forget our first time at autism camp. The camp was held at a local school with the activities coordinated in the gym. The parents were housed in a nearby classroom. The strangeness of the setting, the different activities, being placed in the care of the buddy who was a stranger, and the noise level of all these children together was intimidating, to say the least.

There were a lot of tears and a lot of traffic back and forth between the two rooms. And not all of the tears and traffic were from the kids. If you were an observer that first day, you would have seen parents hovering outside the gym, peeking in the windows, and sitting on the floor right outside, ready at a moment's notice for a summons to their child's side.

No matter where the parents were stationed, they chattered, exchanged tips, and commiserated in regard to issues with insurance, bills, school systems, and inaccessibility to therapy. We discussed the sticky day-to-day issues: potty training, public meltdowns, our other children, the strain on our marriages. We shared the sad and the comedy of our daily lives.

That program is still in effect today and is a testament to these two women's initiative. It is this type of initiative that is necessary at a national level. As a group, we need to raise our voices. Today, many children with autism are not getting the services they need or desire. We know the incidence of autism is rising. We also know that the earlier the intervention, the better the chance the child will reach his or her potential. This means an effective program of therapy and education is the answer. Therefore, we need our school systems to prepare for this influx of children with autism. We also need insurance to cover the diagnosis and treatment. Today, only sixteen states have legislation that mandates that insurance companies provide this type of coverage. We need to make our voices heard through letter-writing campaigns, e-mails, and letters so that the rest of the states follow suit. Our stories are the most powerful tool to aiding our children in their futures.

While I have learned the impact of communication, I believe there are some who need to attend Lorena's classroom. We all have an innate need to comfort and to fix. That is how clichés were born. I understand that this is one of the reasons that people have said some of the stupid things to me that they have. However, I swear that some people just don't use their heads before they speak. I also am convinced that some people don't hear what is coming out of their mouths, because if they heard it like I do, I can't believe they would utter such hurtful statements. Some examples are:

> "Well, maybe she will be really retarded so she doesn't know she is different." I think that was somehow supposed to be comforting.

> "At least she is pretty." Thank God for that, because I didn't want to have to cope with autism *and* ugliness.

> "Just take her home, put her in a corner, and love her, because there isn't much else you are going to be able to do with her." This from a specialist.

And my all-time favorite:

> "I would rather have my child be dead than handicapped." Yep, someone really said that to me.

Are you horrified, because I was, and it was one of the few times in my life I was speechless. I had to go in the bathroom and cry after hearing that last sentiment expressed. I also have to tell you that an acquaintance responded with this statement when she heard the story: "Well, some people feel that way, and you can't blame them." You know what, I understand how you might feel that way, but I don't think I would say that to anyone. I can't imagine how that statement uttered out loud can be construed as appropriate in any circumstances, but maybe that is just me.

I think children handle this whole business the best. They haven't learned all those sticky social rules yet. So their reactions are straightforward. "What is wrong with her?" I don't think that is hurtful at all. It is honest, and they are just trying to understand. I explain, and it is done. Rarely have I had a child make fun or be mean after the explanation.

My favorite example of this occurred at our community pool. Lorena and I are fixtures at the pool during the summer. One day she was playing in the baby pool when another boy her age tried to talk to her. Of course, she didn't look him in the eye or respond. He stood looking puzzled and then marched over to me. "What's wrong with her?" He swung his arm in her direction. I told him she was autistic and couldn't talk, but she could hear and understand. I could see his little brain accept the explanation. He turned around and yelled across the pool, "Hey, Mom, you see that girl? She can't talk." The mother hushed him and worriedly peered over at me. I smiled. He went over and began a running commentary while attempting to draw Lorena into playing with him. At this point, Lorena made one of the noises she is prone to making. He stood up, looked at me, and yelled, "Hey, she can talk. She just did." I explained that she made noises but didn't use words. He scrunched up his face, trying to digest this newest piece of data. He turned and yelled across the pool to his mother, "She can't make words, Mom; she just makes noises." At this point the mother hopped off her chair, waded into the pool, grabbed his arm, and looked at me. "I am so sorry; he ain't right either." I busted out laughing. "He is fine. I would much rather have that than the way other people handle it." I wish everyone wasn't right; it would make it easier. That boy still goes to the pool every summer, and he always talks to Lorena. Again, simple acceptance is so appreciated.

I much prefer this response to the covert glances and puzzled expressions of the parents, who then smile at you when you catch them and pretend they don't notice anything. When I catch someone doing this, I just look at them and say, "She is autistic." I usually get one of a few reactions. Either they nod politely and move away, or they relate to the statement by telling me they know someone who has autism or another disability, or they ask what autism is. A few brave souls will somehow ask tactfully what is wrong with Lorena. I appreciate these dialogues. It is like the elephant in the living room; you can't ignore it, and once everyone knows, it is just easier.

My hope is that someday Lorena will be able to speak for herself; that a scientist will research and find that key to unlock her thoughts. Until then, I don't believe her communication class is dismissed, and we will have to keep learning how to listen and speak for her.

September Tomatoes

My dad loves to garden. He has cleared a large plot of ground at my brother's place. He and my brother have even surrounded the area with an electric fence to keep out the critters that like to nibble at his lettuce, spinach, and broccoli plants. The fresh harvest marks the summer season. I know in June I will have fresh spinach salad, radishes, and broccoli. My coworkers start to hit me up in July, asking, "Does your dad have any extra zucchini?" I know summer is almost over when the tomatoes start arriving. And they arrive by the bushel basket.

Canning is not a simple task. It is hot, heavy work. My Grandma Ruffing left me her pressure cooker. It is a big beast, heavy and old (at least fifty years), and to my son's amusement, I can still get parts for it. He is also amused by my fearful respect of it. My mom told every year how my Grandma Swope had a pressure cooker blow through the ceiling. Therefore, I don't let anyone in the kitchen when mine is steaming away. That is the last step in a long process consisting of lots of scalding water, peeling tomatoes, sterilizing jars, and packing tomatoes into those jars. I have such satisfaction at the end of the day when those jars are filled with plump, red tomatoes and lined up on the counter. I also have to admit I am relieved when Dad drops off his last bushel basket with, "Well, that is it for this year."

It didn't used to be it for me in the years before my Grandpa Gerber died. Grandpa was also an avid gardener, but in his later years he planted his garden a little later than my dad did. Grandpa's tomatoes would arrive in September. I would see his black car bulleting up the drive (he had a heavy foot with the gas pedal). He would get out of the car, a little unsteady on his feet, and proudly carry the fruits of his labor to my door. I would start the process all over. I would call to give him the report at the end of the day—how many quarts of sauce and whole tomatoes. "That's great, honey." I could just hear his pride through the phone line. We would talk about what I would use them for during the winter, and I could tell he was so pleased to have been able to provide for my family. I have to admit, sometimes I wanted to take the whole basket and just chuck them into a field. Today I would give anything to have Grandpa bringing his September tomatoes.

We often take these gestures of family support for granted until they are gone. I know I do, because my Grandpa didn't just support me with fresh produce. He was there for me in so many ways after Lorena was born. She went to therapy four times a week from the time she was eight months old until she entered the school system at age three. These therapy sessions took about three and a half hours by the time we drove her there, participated in therapy, and drove her back home. My mom and dad were still both working full time at this time, I was working nights, and Mike was working evenings. Mike and I took turns hauling Mickey along with us until he started preschool. Then we had to juggle his drop-off and pick-up times with her therapy times. Grandpa Gerber stepped in. He would pick Mickey up and take him out to McDonald's for lunch. Sounds simple enough, but Grandpa lived in the next town, so he would drive twenty minutes to pick Mickey up, eat lunch, and then drive home. He was spending forty minutes on the road to help us for thirty minutes. I don't think he ever realized how much that meant to us and what he gave us. He gave me one less thing on the list to worry about—he helped Mickey have the opportunity to attend preschool, and he taught us that it was okay to ask for help.

You see, that was another lesson I had to learn. *It is okay to need help.* Nurses are notorious for being helpers. As a group, nurses seemed to have skipped the developmental stage where we learned to say no and linger for life in the stage loudly proclaiming, "Me do." I had that firmly down pat. I was fiercely independent, always ready to help others find the answers, pitch in, and do what was needed. I was horrible at saying I needed help, someone else to find the answers, or someone else to pick up the slack, not just physically, but emotionally as well.

Grandpa was there emotionally too. When I was tearful or expressing my despair that all those "nevers" were going to come true, he would quietly state, "I think she will do it." He had such simple faith that it would all work out. I would find him in the chair at his house worrying the rosary beads in his hand, silently praying for her future. His boundless faith calmed me. Somewhere in my mind too I came to realize that although he believed she would walk and talk, he also believed no matter what she did or didn't do, we would be okay.

Okay was a huge concept. I desperately wanted to be okay. I remember when we were first overwhelmed by all that was happening, I called a friend. She was the mother of a high school friend and had a son a few years older than me who had cerebral palsy. She also had six other children. I remember calling her and saying, "Just tell me that we are going to be okay." She reassured me, relating all the ways this son had improved their lives. I found it hard to believe that our situation could improve anything but listened to her words. I also remember this piece of advice: *You need to sleep. If you don't take care of yourself, you will wear yourself out and not live to take care of her as long as you can.*

That advice was probably one of the most important pieces I received and one of the hardest lessons to learn. Mike and I had a lot on our plates. We were trying to find a diagnosis, hauling Lorena to therapy, giving Mickey the attention he needed, working, and I am afraid lastly, trying to be a husband and wife. Take care of ourselves? Where was that going to fit in? We still struggle with this concept. Starting with just getting some sleep.

As the National Autistic Society states, "Learning to sleep through the night is something all children have to do."[9] Every parent of a newborn can share stories of their sleep-deprived state. Usually this situation is resolved sometime in the first year of their child's life. I always get a chuckle when parents are sharing their nightmare stories of when their child started to sleep through the night. "Oh, mine was six months, eight months, and so on." They just look at me when I say, "Lorena was six years old."

That's right, six long years old. At first she didn't sleep because she was so ill with RSV and we were waking her up for breathing treatments, medicine, and just checking on her.

After she recovered, though, she still did not sleep through the night. The National Autistic Society relates that almost all children with autism display some sort of sleep disorder. The sleep disturbance is divided into two types: inability to settle, which is the inability to fall asleep at the appropriate time, and waking, which is waking frequently through the night. Lorena displayed both types.

I would like to say that we approached this in an organized manner and have advice for you on weathering this problem. But we didn't and don't; we spent the six years exhausted, cat napping at two- to three-hour intervals and poking each other, saying, "It's your turn to go put her back to bed." The event that finally made us seek professional help was my transferring to day shift. I took Lorena to the doctor and discussed her lack of sleep and ours. I joked with him, "Somebody needs drugs, and I really don't care if it is her or me." He laughed and discussed our options. I ran to the drugstore.

That night, through the magic of chemistry, Lorena fell asleep easily and slept through the night. I would like to say we did too, but we were so used to interrupted nights that we both woke up and checked on her frequently. I went to work, and Mike called at nine a.m. to tell me she was still asleep. And then at noon, still sleeping, and then at one p.m., panicked: "I can't wake her up."

"Is she breathing?"

"Yeah."

"She must really need the sleep."

Lorena woke up at four p.m. I think the poor kid was just as sleep deprived as we were. I debated that night about giving her the medication but decided it was okay to go ahead. It took us a few days, but soon we began to sleep through the night too. I also realized that we should have tried to get professional help sooner. I think that was a support system I often didn't tap quickly enough. Some was based on my previous experience with the various specialists. Some, I admit, was professional pride. Some was that we had spent so much of her earlier years in the doctor's office and hospital, so I avoided them if we could. And a great deal was denial; if we didn't admit it to the doctor, it wasn't happening.

I learned the importance of a family physician as a support. I think the field of autism has grown, and I also believe that there are specialists who are educated in autism and provide help to their patients. I firmly believe, though, that a good family physician can provide holistic care for the whole family. At least ours did. He didn't just ask about Lorena when he saw her, but the whole family. He also didn't just ask about her development delays, but any issues or concerns the family had. I found that as our history as physician and patient grew, we were able to find answers for our family that were the best for us all. In addition, I was able to take options—potential diagnosis, treatments, research—and discuss them with him. I encourage everyone—not just families with children with disabilities—to find a general practitioner and establish this support system.

The other support system I did and still do rely on heavily is my parents. I am lucky. I live and work in the town where I was born. We have never lived more than four miles from my parents' house. My dad retired early, which was a huge benefit for us. Any working mother will tell you the worst part of working is making sure that her children are safe and cared for while she is at work, especially those disruptions in the normal, such as school delays or cancellations. I live with the knowledge that if school is delayed or canceled I don't even have to call anyone or make one arrangement. My dad or mom will be at the door in plenty of time for me to get to work. I also know that if I have a sick child, the same will be true.

They have taken my children for evenings, nights, and weekends to give us a break. They have cooked, cleaned, and done household chores so we had time for the other priorities in our lives—therapy, doctor appointments, Mickey. They read and talked to others and relayed information to try to help us find the answers we were looking for. And they prayed. They listened to us cry and whine. And they gave us tough love.

When Lorena was five, she started to pull her hair out strand by strand one day. I kept telling her no and pulling her hand down. She got on the bus in the morning with a full head of curly hair. When she got off the bus in the afternoon, she was entirely bald on the top of her head. She looked like Benjamin Franklin. The bus aide hovered behind her as she descended the step and then handed me a handful of Lorena's hair. "She did this on the bus ride home. We couldn't get her to stop." I don't know what she was thinking: here's Lorena and here's her hair. I don't know if she thought I could glue it back on or make a wig or what. I was devastated. Lorena had a beautiful head of curly hair. I loved to play with it, adding bright ribbons and bows. I stood there with her hair in my hand and started to bawl. I walked into the house and straight to the phone. "Mom, Lorena pulled her hair all out. I just don't know if I can do this anymore. I just can't take it." And she answered, "Well, you are going to have to."

Huh? Where was my sympathy? How dare she tell me I was going to have to take it. But you know what? She was right. That was another lesson. *I had a choice to take it or not to take it.* After all, I had read about parents giving up their children with disabilities for foster care because they just couldn't emotionally or financially support them. I couldn't imagine making that choice, but I know some did. We also had a children's home for children with disabilities right in our town. Another choice I couldn't imagine making. So I did have to take it, because my choice was to continue to care for Lorena right in our home, and that meant no matter what happened.

So after sniffling and wallowing, I called her back and we talked about how to handle it. I knew Lorena liked to "be pretty." If you said she was pretty, she just preened. So I put her in front of the mirror and kept pointing at her head and telling her that her hair being gone was ugly. Then I stuck a ski cap on her, with all the hair tucked up inside so she couldn't get at her hair, and watched her like a hawk. Okay, so a psychologist probably would have issues with me telling her it was ugly, but it worked and she stopped doing it.

My dad is more of a stoic person. While Mom might cry with me and talk about feelings, Dad was more of an action person. He showed his support. The one story that still makes me laugh is the white Valentine candy. Lorena loved those little candy hearts that appear in the store around Valentine's Day, but she would only eat the white ones. Who knows why?

My Dad is a big guy—six feet two inches—and he likes a good meal. He was in the Navy and still has that straight military bearing. He was a cop on the Norfolk and Southern Railroad until his retirement, which adds to this presence. Lastly, he is prone to voicing his opinions in booming baritone for all to hear. Add all that together, and he is an imposing figure. On one of his weekly grocery shopping trips, he noted the bin of bulk Valentine hearts. He patiently picked through the bin until he had a bag of only white hearts for his granddaughter. A clerk approached him and asked what he was doing. He patiently explained who they were for and why. Knowing Dad, I am sure this was stated in his most intimidating tone, just daring the clerk to question him. I would have loved to be a fly on the wall for that exchange.

I could write pages of these stories. We received this kind of support from my brother and his family, my aunts, my uncles, cousins. They were just there, and I realized that what we had been told by my friend was true. Lorena had brought us closer and we were a better family because of her.

I know that we are lucky. We no longer live in a nation where several generations live under one roof, down the block, or at least in the same town, much less zip code as our immediate family. Our family just happened to all be in close proximity geographically. However, I do see families that live in proximity and still don't support each other. I have heard grandparents say, "Hey, we raised our kids, so don't expect me to be the babysitter." We appreciate the fact that our family is willing to lend a helping hand. I also recognize that family today is often not a blood connection but a choice through work or friendship. I have been doubly blessed; I have this family by choice too.

My coworkers gave me endless support. They traded days so I could take Lorena to her various appointments. They researched with me to try to find a diagnosis. They listened to me whine and complain. They also told me when I had done enough whining and complaining and it was time to shape up. They also made me laugh in that sick, inappropriate way only nurses can understand.

We also benefited from the formal support systems. The first therapists Lorena had were at Early Intervention. Those therapists were our lifelines at the beginning. We saw them once a week for two and a half years. They did the therapy not only with Lorena, but also with us. We would walk into that room, and there would be children with a variety of diagnoses and disabilities. Those therapists—speech, occupational, physical—would plot out a plan of care and goals for each of our children and then take the time to teach each of us how to reach those goals. The Early Intervention room was packed, and *packed* is a good word because everything was in one room at one time—parents, children, therapists, toys, equipment, tips, tears, and laughter.

This is also when I learned that Lorena would also have choices about her therapy and how it would be done. We figured out that she preferred to work with therapists that had blonde hair. The speech therapist had dark hair, and Lorena would not cooperate with her at all. She would cry. We thought it was because it was speech therapy, which was obviously a difficult area for her, until we began to notice that she would not go to or cooperate with people who had dark hair. We had no rhyme or reason for this behavior, but it was very obvious. The speech therapist used to tease that she was going to start to wear a blonde wig so Lorena would go to her. She also would not go to my aunt Debbie, who had dark hair, until my aunt became pregnant with my cousin Annie. Lorena loves babies and once she figured out my aunt had produced one, all was well.

The Early Intervention therapists were the ones who suggested that Lorena needed more therapy than was possible there. We have a local rehabilitation facility with an outstanding reputation. During that time they had just begun to see pediatric patients. So Lorena began therapy there three times a week. Individual therapy was a different atmosphere. We were used to the "groupthink" in Early Intervention. At individual therapy, Lorena went into therapy and we sat in the waiting area. I would take cross-stitch, crochet, a book, and wait. Mike would head to the cafeteria for the giant cinnamon rolls. We usually didn't go together because one of us would stay home with Mickey if we could, or if I was working, Mike would take Mickey until he entered preschool.

While the quiet time was nice, I began to have a problem while waiting for Lorena. I swear I have "confess to me" written on my forehead. I am sure it is a nursing thing, because I would be in the waiting room and people would come in to wait. Pretty soon, I was listening to life stories, offering reassurance and Kleenex. I decided at one point that I just couldn't do this anymore. There were days I was barely holding myself together, much less anyone else, so I hunted around until I found a different, hidden place to wait by myself.

Individual therapy was beneficial for Lorena's physical and occupational therapy, but I didn't feel supported. Appointments were back-to-back, so the therapists were kind but couldn't devote time to our issues. It made it harder to go there because I felt so isolated. This therapy schedule, on top of work, family, and other obligations, was time consuming.

When I look back now, it seems as though that time from her birth to three years old happened in the blink of an eye. At three, Lorena was to transition to the local school system. It was time for some decisions. We were given several options: a) attend the county mental retardation/development delay program (MR/DD); b) sign up for one of the preschools in our area; c) enroll her in the county program for children of low-income families—Lorena's disability qualified her for this program; or d) a combination of any of the programs.

Enrolling Lorena in one of these programs was a definite dose of reality. We could not deny her delays at this point. She was not potty trained, was nonverbal, still wasn't walking alone, and didn't play interactively. I was so grateful for the other parents and therapists in Early Intervention because they helped us debate the pros and cons.

Mickey attended a local Lutheran preschool. We loved that school. They had a Christian philosophy, and the emphasis was on learning to be good people. I also liked the fact that they believed in fun and not pushing the kids to be geniuses at age two. It was more about socializing and learning solid values. It was heartbreaking to realize that Lorena was not going to be able to follow in her brother's footsteps as easily as his peers' siblings were. The director of the school was a speech therapist who worked in the public school system too. I casually mentioned to her that Lorena would be starting preschool and probably would not be able to come to this preschool. That good woman insisted she could.

It was then I learned the difference between a job and a calling. Those teachers truly felt it was their Christian duty to teach all children and help them be the best they could become as individuals. They blew all my worries away. Not potty trained? We can deal with that. Doesn't walk? Okay. And they had been signing in class before Lorena ever attended, so they just kept doing it. And the kids were wonderful. They just didn't know to treat her any differently. In fact, I know therapy had a lot to do with it, but I swear Lorena started walking because of two little girls in her class. They would each hold her hands and say, "Come on, Wena, let's go." And she would toddle between them until she was toddling on her own.

The public school program was not as wonderful. It wasn't that they didn't try, because they did. But, there were a lot of kids with a lot of needs. It was here that I learned that poverty is its own disability. Most of the mothers were very young or uneducated. I saw very few fathers, and the day I decided this was the wrong program for Lorena was the day we were walking through the hallway and Lorena brushed up against a child. The mother pulled her daughter to herself, as if Lorena were contagious. Don't get me wrong; these programs have a place and give the students great opportunities, but it was not the niche for my child.

We went back to the local MR/DD where the Early Intervention program had been. This program had a mix of typical kids and kids with disabilities, so I knew Lorena would get a mix of interaction. Lorena would still attend the Lutheran preschool and this program. One of the big challenges, though, was transportation. I had to put my three-year-old on a bus.

I don't know why exactly that was so difficult, but for some reason, putting that non-walking child on the bus was terrifying. I think there is a difference between the picture of a typical child at the age of five going to kindergarten, happily skipping out to the bus, and Lorena crying and clinging, being handed to an aide to be carried to her seat on the bus. She looked so tiny and defenseless. I knew this was the right choice, but it still made my gut clench.

The public system is one formal support system we have now been in for fifteen years. We have had some successes and we have had some failures. I decided when Lorena turned four that I should start planning on where she would go. I didn't know where to start, so I started with the superintendent, who referred me to the school psychologist. I explained Lorena's delays and asked what type of programs were available.

And this educated man who was going to help me find the right spot for my child stated, "Well, we really don't have a classroom she could fit in here. Besides, we have a hard time getting teachers for these kinds of kids; they just get tired of teaching them." I suddenly knew firsthand what it meant to "see red." I was furious. I don't really remember what I said, because it is in a cloud of mind-numbing anger, but I know I refuted what he said, cited many examples of teachers we had encountered so far who had worked with "these children" for years, and a couple other not nice statements. I then returned to the superintendent, who told me that he was sure I had "misunderstood."

Needless to say, we decided that Lorena should continue at our local MR/DD school—School of Hope (SOH)—for kindergarten. However, the teachers there kept encouraging us to try to mainstream Lorena. The SOH principal discussed the fact that she felt the kids that were now attending the school were not at the level Lorena was and that she would benefit more from mainstreaming. They felt that a typical school with typical kids would benefit her. What I didn't realize at the time was that mainstreaming was a fairly new concept. Pardini relates that the government mandated school attendance in 1918. However, children with disabilities were routinely excluded and either stayed home or were institutionalized. In 1975, the Education for All Handicapped Children Act was passed (2002)[10]. This act has evolved over the years into the Individuals with Disabilities Education Act. These laws outlined the basis for Individual Education Plans (IEPs), funding (although the federal government has never lived up to its promises), and the least restrictive environment (Martin, Martin, & Terman, 1996).[11]

This means that the idea of educating children in public school systems was only recognized nationwide thirty years ago. So special education is a fairly young concept. I'd say from firsthand experience that school systems are still struggling with this concept. It begins with funding. The federal government agreed with the first act in 1975 to provide monies for 40 percent of special education monies. To date, the federal government provides 15 percent (Pardini, 2002). Special education is costly.

According to the Department of Education, approximately six million children (roughly 10 percent of all school-aged children) receive special education services. Educating those children was expected to cost nearly $51 billion last year, according to the Department of Education's Center for Special Education Finance, with the yeoman's share—more than $44 billion—coming from states and local school districts" (Pardini, 2002).

I have also found personally that schools struggle with the concept of least-restrictive environment. I understand their struggle. Lorena was nonverbal, used minimal signs, had trouble with fine and gross motor skills, and did not transition well. The standardized tests they had given Lorena showed her well below normal mentally, although I knew and the school personnel admitted that they were not an accurate measurement. We did know from her previous experience in preschool with typical kids that she did seem to benefit from interaction with typical kids. I also recognize even today that I was still searching for normal and wanted her to be in a normal school, following in her typical brother's footsteps.

I try to look at this from a teacher's perspective, though. Average classroom size at that time was around twenty students. I don't know how you balance the special needs of a child with twenty typical children. And just because these children are typical does not mean they are all functioning at the same level of development. So this teacher has to balance all these needs while making sure that the curriculum goals for the year are met.

Lorena entered kindergarten in the mid-nineties, so mainstreaming really was fairly new. I remember discussing with the MR/DD superintendent what would be least restrictive for her and still promote her growth. She felt very strongly that it would be best for Lorena to be in her home school district. I agreed. However, what I didn't realize was that our school district did not have a classroom for her. By then they had hired a person to be the liaison for special education students. He recommended that Lorena not attend the MR/DD program but still be in the county special education classroom and mainstreamed as much as possible. Sounds good, right? Except this county classroom moved every year to whatever building had room for them. The first year, the classroom was in the next town over. She had to ride the bus, and since they picked up kids all over Bellevue, she ended up being on the bus for an hour and a half both going to school and coming home. The mainstreaming wasn't what I thought either. The first year, she didn't leave the classroom because they thought she would be disruptive. The second year, she went to music.

I began to think about this. In my mind, that is not what mainstreaming meant. It is not mainstreaming if you are in a regular school but don't interact in a typical situation with the rest of the kids. See some red flags here? Kids with autism don't transition well and need help adjusting to change. I tried to find out at the end of the school year when we had her IEP meetings where she would be the next year, and would get the same song and dance every year. "Well, it depends on funding and class availability. We'll let you know as soon as we can." One year I called in August and demanded to know where she was going. They finally could tell me August 15, two weeks before she was to start school. I also asked them if she could at least see the classroom and meet the teacher before she began. The various personnel at the school politely explained that teachers don't arrive at school until a few days before it starts, they are busy getting ready for the year, and so on. I was so frustrated I just wanted to scream.

In addition, Lorena hated the bus ride. It was incredibly long, she didn't like the bus, and she was the last child to leave the school at the end of the day. Every year I would discuss this busing situation and would hear, "Well, we have a lot of kids over a large area. We do the best we can." Her teacher called me her second year in the public system and related that Lorena was absolutely screaming when the buses started to pick kids up. The teacher felt that Lorena was afraid they weren't taking her home. The teacher also related that they had tried to discuss with the bus coordinator how upset Lorena was. The final note was that the bus was sitting at another school waiting to pick up those kids whose dismissal time was later, and that was why Lorena was picked up last.

I decided enough was enough. I called the bus coordinator and got the same song and dance the teacher had gotten. I lost it. I used the F word and told her, "Don't f*** with me. I don't understand why you can't pick her up first if the bus is sitting at another school. Then go to the school that is dismissed later and pick up the other kids." The coordinator told me that they would look at the situation. I'm not proud of the way I acted, but it was effective. Lorena's teacher called me about twenty minutes later and told me she didn't know what I had done, but they had just gotten a call that the bus schedule would be changed that day. Lorena was happy, no more crying, the teacher was happy, and I had learned another lesson, *sometimes you just need to find the mean within to get what is needed.*

Unfortunately, the next few years, Lorena was placed in county classroom two towns over that just did not help her develop. I hated that school. First of all, it held this classroom and classrooms for the children with severe behavior problems. You could just feel the negative atmosphere when you walked in. The teacher also was not very creative and I don't think set the standard very high, so Lorena did not progress. She also learned at this school how to fake being sick. I can't tell you how many times I would get a call saying Lorena was laying on the floor, lethargic and nodding yes when they asked if she was sick. No fever but obviously was ill. I would go get her, and on the way home this ill child would be giggling and bouncing in her seat.

I went back to the school administration with my new knowledge about being demanding and flatly told them they needed to figure out a different placement because she was not going back there. I didn't know that I was really right, because that school was no longer going to be available the next year. So again Lorena was going to be transferred to another classroom. This time, though, we hit the jackpot.

Her next teacher was one of the most creative, extraordinary teachers I have encountered. She saw the real child with all the potential and the reality of her disability. She took the time to educate herself in regard to autism and figured out how to help Lorena. The aides in the classroom were also extraordinary, and this teaching team helped Lorena make huge strides forward. For instance, this teacher was the one who effectively began to use picture schedules. She was the one who helped Lorena communicate through pictures and signs more effectively. She was also the one who figured out how to motivate Lorena. She taught Lorena by rewarding her for right answers with the motivation that meant the most to

Lorena—being pretty. She videotaped one of their lessons. Lorena would pick the correct answer, and she would get a pretty bow in her hair. But if she picked the wrong answer, Mrs. Mills got the pretty bow in her hair. You had to see the picture of this teacher sitting with this disarray of ribbons in her hair. It worked, though.

I will never forget their first Christmas program. My mom and dad went with me, and I saw that Lorena was the narrator and was going to introduce the class. I thought, *Now how is that going to happen?* Well, Mrs. Mills read the students' names, and Lorena would go up to each student and give them a high-five as their name was announced. She also was the prop master and helped hand out props as the story played out. I was so proud of Lorena and her skills that day.

I admired that teacher and her skills more than I can say. She not only helped Lorena progress; she restored my faith in the school system. She was the formal support I had desired from the school system. Until that point I always felt defensive with anyone in the school system, as though I was constantly defending Lorena's potential and worth. I always felt as though the school system viewed her as a burden they had to deal with. Now I felt again that she had a place in this system and it was their job to help her be all she could be.

She stayed with Mrs. Mills for a few years and then, to my great dismay, had to move on. We again debated on the proper setting. At this time I made the difficult decision to move her back to the MR/DD school. We made this choice for several reasons. One, I was trying to keep an eye on her future. The MR/DD school had a workshop for adults. When I thought about Lorena, her well-being, and her future, I felt that this work setting was probably the most appropriate. I also knew that the middle and high school that Lorena would be placed in was in a town where there was gang activity that our town does not have. It was also a huge school, and I was fearful for her security.

At age eighteen, she had attended this school for five years and began to transition into the workshop. I think this was the right decision. Again, she has been lucky enough to have teachers and aides who are creative and see her potential. Both she and we are supported.

I think this story would be different if Lorena were entering the school system today. I know that our community school system has had tremendous growth in meeting special needs. I know of several children with autism who are currently mainstreamed into our local system. And when I say mainstreamed, I mean they are in a typical classroom with an aide, functioning at their optimal level. But we have made the best decisions we could in the system we have, and sometimes that is all you can do.

God Ain't No Santa Claus

I was raised a good Catholic. We attended church weekly without fail. Didn't eat meat on Fridays during Lent. My brother and I made all the sacraments as children, culminating in our confirmation. My mom regularly went to Bingo. I fell away from the church, as teens do, when I went to nursing school. I stopped attending weekly Mass, ate meat on Fridays during Lent, stopped going to confession, and I hated Bingo. When I married Mike, who was not Catholic, this downhill slide continued. My mother expressed her disapproval verbally, while lighting candles and praying quietly. The birth of my son, Mickey, prompted her to take a much more active role. I am sure my father and she were convinced that I was going to raise my children in this heathen lifestyle. So, they arranged to pick us up for church and would bribe us with a meal at our favorite local restaurant after church. I think Mike liked this arrangement, because he slept in late and met us for the meal. It was a win-win for all.

This pattern continued after Lorena's birth, with one major difference. Before her birth, I attended church and actually enjoyed the ceremony—the peace, the quiet. Even if I didn't always listen actively, I was often reflecting, which I felt was a kind of personal prayer. I also liked the singing. I have a fairly strong voice and can carry a tune. When I was younger, a nun made a deep impression on me when she told me that God had given me this voice and I always needed to use it to honor Him.

After Lorena's birth and subsequent illness and delays, I attended the Mass in stony silence. You see, God and I were no longer on speaking or singing terms. I was so angry with Him for letting this happen to me. After all, I had been a good girl. I mean, I had broken a few of the Big Ten rules, lied occasionally, not always honored the Sabbath, didn't always obey my parents. But, I had never committed the biggies, you know, like murder. Therefore, I was pretty sure that I did not deserve what was happening to me. And, God was just not living up to His part of the bargain.

I kept going, though, because I was afraid not to. Spiritually, I was a mess. I had been taught that God would provide comfort and support in times of trouble, yet I was in the greatest turmoil of my life and felt the most abandoned. We have all heard of the miraculous cures that many faithful experience. I was fearful that part of the reason for a lack of cure for Lorena was due to my anger and lack of faith in God.

I also felt rejected by my church community. We did not take Lorena to church during her extended illness with RSV. I didn't want to expose her to other bugs at church, and she was receiving breathing treatments around the clock. I did start to take her after she recovered from the illness. She did not tolerate church well.

She would be fine when we entered the church. As soon as the organ music started, she would begin to cry. I know now that because of her tactile defensiveness the sound was actually painful. At that time, I didn't understand. She also had developed this terrible habit of tearing little pieces of the prayer books. I would take the book from her, and she would begin to scream. Again, I realize now that the behavior was an autistic behavior that helped to calm her. I just thought then she was being destructive, and it was unacceptable. I would try to give her a bottle or snacks to distract her. Sometimes this worked; sometimes this did not. Then the clucking would start. No, not from Lorena, but from my fellow parishioners. Whispers, glares, and tsking. I knew what they were thinking: *Why doesn't she make that child behave? What kind of mother is she?* I even had a few ask me, "Why do you bring her to church?"

Why did I? First of all, I was still clinging to that hope of a miracle, so I was trying to be good. And I thought if she were in church, maybe God would make it happen. Secondly, I started to get mad. Did she not have just as much right as anyone else in church? How dare they say we shouldn't be in church. How Christian was that? Lastly, I began to figure out that if I removed Lorena from uncomfortable situations, she learned to act up to get out. Eventually she quit ripping the books; she would not start crying at the organ music until the third song. Gradually, she just began to tolerate church. It was not a quick process; it took a few years to get to this point.

My anger and feelings of rejection grew during that time. I could not find faith, I could not find peace, and I could not let go of the idea that I did not deserve this punishment I was sure God had ordained. Then one day I had an epiphany. Not in church, but in my kitchen at home, listening to *Rudolph the Red-Nosed Reindeer*.

Lorena loves that movie. I have watched it hundreds of time in my life. This time was different, though. I was in the kitchen baking cookies. Lorena was four and re-watching *Rudolph* for the millionth time in a row. The video had only played for a couple minutes and was to the scene where Santa was meeting Rudolph for the first time. He was actually telling Rudolph's dad that he would never be accepted or be able to be one of his reindeer. I remember thinking, *Santa is a bigot*. I had never realized before that in this children's show, Santa is not a very nice person. I went into the living room and actually watched the show. Suddenly, the characters had new meaning.

Rudolph's parents were Mike and me. We struggled with Lorena's disability. At first we denied it was happening. Then we did our best to accept the disability. I hoped that we, unlike Rudolph's parents, did not make her feel like a burden. Hermy was all those other parents of children with disabilities and their children. We were all trying to be "independent together," reaching out to each other, supporting, and educating each other along the way. The Island of Misfit Toys was the various meetings and support groups Mike and I attended, trying to find where we fit. Then there was Yukon Cornelius. He was my parents, family, friends, therapists, and our family physician—everyone who gave us a lift and supported us along our way. I also realized that autism was the Abominable Snow Monster, Bumble. Autism was big and scary, taking a huge bite out of our life. Many times we felt as though our life was falling over a cliff, never to return to normal. But somehow, we bounced. And like the

Bumble, who puts the star on the tree, Autism had taught us new abilities and strengths.

The greatest revelation was that I had been thinking of God as Santa Claus. I wanted him to be a benevolent human being who gave me whatever I had on my Christmas list. When I didn't get what I wanted, I stopped speaking to him. I also realized that of all the characters, Clarice was the most God-like. She just loved and supported Rudolph the way he was. She sought him out when he avoided her, and she was willing to risk herself to help Rudolph.

I thought about what I had realized, and I also thought about what I had been taught. Another light bulb went off: God had not done this to me. I wasn't being punished. Sometimes things did just happen for no rhyme or reason. I knew from being a nurse how frail the human body was. It probably is a miracle that the majority of us are "normal" or even survive as long as we do. I also recognized that I had thought I just did not have enough faith, when actually the opposite was true. I had met each obstacle over the last four years head on, and we, including Lorena, continued to progress and grow. I had faith—faith that we could overcome these obstacles and be okay. I also believed we were able to do this because of gifts we had been given from the start: Mike's sense of humor and sensitivity; Mickey's compassionate, sunny nature; my stubborn personality and knowledge. How could you not believe in a higher power with all that working for you?

I would like to say my feud with God ended right then and I was able to go to church from then on with no hard feelings. It wasn't quite that easy. I had been hanging on to that anger for too long to just let it go instantly. I also still harbored anger at what I felt was a hostile environment at church. We had a young priest at that time, and he actively sought me out. He came to our home a few times for dinner. He assured me we were all welcome. He also emphasized that Lorena should take part in church in any way she could. I also suspect that he was doing some background education with the parishioners. The parishioners began to shake my hand during the sign of the peace and would sometimes lightly touch Lorena to include her. One fellow parishioner gave Lorena a Christmas present and said we needed to keep bringing her special little self to church. I was so touched. Slowly, the clucks became understanding smiles when Lorena acted out in church.

One Christmas Eve, Lorena was having a particularly difficult time sitting through Mass. She always becomes over stimulated at the holidays, and I could tell we were heading for a meltdown. She was hitting her head and crying. I was rubbing her back and trying to shush her. The woman behind me leaned over, touched my shoulder, and said, "It's okay; you are among friends." Lorena wasn't the only one crying then.

The young priest left the parish, to my sorrow, and another priest took his place. By now, Lorena was tolerating Mass fairly well. She would always walk up to Communion with me, and when she turned ten, she began to put her hand out for the Communion wafer too. I would hold her hand, and we would move back to the pew. Our former pastor had told us Lorena should be able to make all the sacraments. I called our new pastor and explained the situation. I was especially concerned by the fact that she couldn't say "Amen" when receiving the host. I know this sounds ridiculous, but sometimes it is the simplest concerns that take on the biggest implications. He reassured me in the best possible way, "Lorena has made her intentions clear. Let God take care of the rest."

We chose to have Lorena make her first Communion in May at a Mass by herself. She was invited to make it with the class that year, but I thought the whole thing might be too much for her. The Catholic Christian Doctrine (CCD) teacher gave me videos for her to watch. Father met privately with us for her to practice. He gave her the host to taste, and she chewed it. He then asked me, "Is it okay if she has a bit of the creature too?" I nodded yes. He gave Lorena the chalice with wine and turned his back to put the bottle on the counter. She drank the whole amount. And then signed for more. I started cracking up.

Of course, from a girl's standpoint, one of the most important parts of First Communion is the dress. I decided to cut down my wedding dress and make Lorena's dress out of it. I was a little intimidated by the project, though. I found a seamstress who was willing to do this. She was so kind, measuring and fitting Lorena. The dress came out beautifully, and she looked like a miniature bride with her white veil and flowing dress.

We invited all our extended family for the event. At the beginning of Mass, Father announced that this was a special occasion. He explained that Lorena was making her First Communion. He also explained autism and ended by saying that even though she couldn't speak, she had demonstrated her faith too. I was so grateful to him. She was absolutely perfect during Mass that day. The big moment came, and she proudly walked up to the altar. Father raised his hand holding the host and said, "The Body of Christ." Lorena nodded her head yes and took the host. I was so proud of her. The whole event overwhelmed. Here, at last, was a piece of normal to hang on to, and I also felt that this was another step to our acceptance in our religious community.

Spiritually, I felt that she and I had come a long way. I also think the experience prompted me to consciously seek faith. I began to read about religion and faith. One story on Buddhism particularly prompted me to look at my beliefs. The way I understand Buddhism is that you "earn" your next life by the way you act in this one. I hope I have not misrepresented this and do not wish to offend anyone, but I find that concept fascinating.

Sometimes I am jealous of Lorena. You think I am crazy, right? I know at times she has anxiety mostly related to her inability to communicate on our level, but I also think she is lucky in many ways. Basically, she is loved, fed, sheltered, and her needs are consistently met. She does not have the day-to-day stress of living like us in the normal world. I look at that, given the Buddhist point of view, and think maybe she earned this in a past life. Maybe she had reached her ultimate being and so this time she gets to go through life taken care of by us. And we become better people by taking care of her. I don't know what that says about the way we must have lived our past lives. I see this, though, with every person she encounters. I have described the effect she has had on our family and the greater community. And the lesson I learned is that *her life has purpose and meaning; this child is changing the world for the better.*

Total Eclipse of the Sun

A total eclipse occurs when the moon passes between the sun and the earth. Scientists teach us not to view an eclipse directly because if you do, you will burn your eyes and cause blindness. They also teach you that the way to view an eclipse is to construct a pinhole viewer, which lets you indirectly view it without burning your eyes. I think I use that same technique when viewing Lorena's autism. I know that if I look directly at the whole picture, I become overwhelmed and blind to any solutions. But if I look at it through a pinhole, highlighting pieces of it, I can deal with each piece without going blind.

This is my coping mechanism. I also understand that this mechanism is part of the whole grieving process. I think most people have heard of the Kubler-Ross stages of death and dying—denial, anger, bargaining, depression, and acceptance. I don't think most people understand that we don't just grieve death. We also grieve with events in our lives. We can grieve the loss of income, of health, a divorce. We can also grieve positive events. For instance, a person can be thrilled with a new promotion on the job but grieve the loss of the status quo; the changing relationship with coworkers. Or a couple could grieve the loss of "coupleness" with the birth of a new child. In any of these situations, the person is able to work through the grief process with the end result of resolution.

In my case, I was grieving the loss of the normal child I had envisioned. Mike and I chose not to find out the gender of our children with either of my pregnancies. I had witnessed births during nursing school, and that moment when the doctor held the baby and announced, "It's a girl or boy," was always thrilling. The parents' indescribable joy was a memory I carried with me, and I wanted that surprise moment with my husband in the delivery room. I spent the entire pregnancy hypothesizing which flavor of child I would have.

I also submitted to the various wives' tale tests my friends and families put me through. I put up with the comments about carrying all my weight in my butt or my belly being low or high or round, which indicated a boy or a girl, depending on the predictor. And I took a bite of bread with a needle stuck in it: a bite at the pointed end meant a boy, the eye end, a girl. I don't remember which end I bit, but I do remember having morning sickness and the bread increasing my nausea. And of course, I lay on the couch while friends and family suspended needles on strings over my rotund belly.

Every time someone issued their particular prediction, I would daydream about my child. A boy certainly would be a football player. After all, our men are large and assertive. A girl brought forth visions of ballet lessons and pink tutus. Either child in this dream was brilliant: a future valedictorian, lawyer, doctor. I never envisioned a child not in perfect health.

I went into the labor room to deliver Lorena thinking it would be just great if Mickey got a sister. Our little family would be perfect: a mommy, a daddy, one son, and one daughter. I was so enamored of this idea that Mike and I barely thought about a boy's name. I remember being absolutely thrilled when I heard those magic words, "It's a girl!"

I grieved the loss of these visions, the loss of my hopes and dreams. I experienced the denial and have discussed my avoidance of the reality. Bargaining went hand in hand with the denial. I have discussed how angry I became at doctors, therapists, teachers, anyone who stood in the way of what I thought we needed or what would "fix" Lorena. I had always thought that people who were grieving and in the stage of anger were mad at God. I didn't understand that you could just be mad. That the emotion of anger could take on a life of its own.

Anger is very protective because your target is always someone else or something else. I couldn't get mad at Lorena, this innocent child, so I took my anger out on others— coworkers, friends, family, strangers. I learned that people didn't always react when you were polite or sad, but boy did people move when you were irate. I did begin to realize that I didn't like myself in this constant state of anger. There was no happiness when you were constantly ticked off.

Once I couldn't deny the reality any longer or I chose not to be angry, I had periods of great sadness. It was debilitating and scary. I had no energy. I often felt like I was walking through sucking swamp mud. I was physically exhausted anyway because of the broken sleep pattern I had because of Lorena, and my depression zapped the rest of my energy. The alarm clock would go off in the morning, and I would have to talk myself into getting up, taking a shower, caring about how I looked, getting dressed, driving to work, working. Everything took a monumental amount of effort.

On top of that, I had trouble thinking clearly. I couldn't remember anything. The scariest episode was one time when I went to the grocery store. I walked into the store, stood, and couldn't quite remember where I was and what I was there to get. I remember starting to cry and being afraid that I really had lost my mind. The seconds ticked by. I don't know how long I stood there fighting for control. I took several deep breaths and backtracked in my head to why I had come to the store. I finally remembered what I needed, got it, and got out of the store.

People have often asked me if I was suicidal during this time. I just didn't have enough energy to care about myself. Yet I didn't want to die; I just wanted to be voted off the island for a while. I wanted to go someplace where I didn't have to deal with anything. I wanted my "normal" life back, where I was sure of everything, where I had my life laid out exactly as planned. My organized soul just could not deal with the chaos autism was causing.

Eventually, as anyone who grieves does, I began to reach resolution, a new normal where I was comfortable with my current situation. I found that first I would have just a couple hours where I could laugh again, where every minute was not consumed by Lorena and autism. Then I began to have whole days, then two days in a row, and then a week. I discovered, as these periods of wellness got longer, that I didn't sink as low into the swamp muck again. And I actually began to realize that I had some control over my raging emotions. I would simply get busy with hobbies or cleaning or cooking to stop thinking about it. Work became a permanent escape hatch, especially because I worked in the intensive care unit, where the patients and family desperately needed me to be attentive. The lesson I learned was that *I did have some control and choice.* I could choose to live miserable in the muck or find the joy and the positive. I choose the joy.

However, I didn't realize that parents of a child with a disability don't ever resolve grief completely. Chronic sorrow, first described by Olshansky, is the cyclical, recurring grief or sadness of parents or caregivers that occurs with different degrees of intensity at various times during the lifetime of an individual with a serious or chronic condition (Hobdell, 2004)[12]. I found that I would have triggers that would set the grief cycle again. For instance, Christmas is always difficult. I would be standing in the store buying gifts for Lorena with labels clearly stating for a "child twelve months and under" or "one to three years," and she would be six or seven. These labels were black-and-white reminders of her delays. It made me sad and took some of the fun out of the shopping—not that I am overjoyed with shopping to begin with any time. Until the year I went shopping with my aunt Debbie. She didn't let me agonize over every choice, trying to pick the toys that would help Lorena develop. She just tossed toys and dolls and stuff in the cart. And suddenly it was fun again. I still get a little sad every year, but shopping is no longer a major obstacle.

Another event that slaps reality in my face is her birthday. Every year brings those milestones. I realized after a few years that from June until August I was in a funk thinking about all the things Lorena couldn't do—especially when her brother was just eighteen months older. He turned five and marched off to kindergarten; Lorena turned five and we spent the year before debating about appropriate placement. He turned ten and began to use hair gel and whisper with friends about girls with cooties. She turned ten and we were still trying to get her completely potty trained. He turned the dreaded thirteen and was a teenager with a cell phone, Nintendo, and sleepovers. She turned thirteen and had none of that. She will be nineteen in 2010. He has his license, is attending college, and has a major. We still have to look for a companion for Lorena in the summer when she is not at the workshop or attending camp. This is a huge disparity, but I have found that instead of focusing on everything she is not doing, I get sad but concentrate on her progress.

For instance, the bus pulls up to our house and she walks up to it by herself with a smile on her face. She is no longer that weeping heap I used to lug out to the bus. Her communication has grown, and she makes her wants and needs known. She is particular about her clothes and hair, just like any typical teenager. She has friends in school and even got friendly with one boy this year. Now that was scary, but oh too normal!

The triggers that are harder to handle are the ones that take me off guard. For instance, Mike and I were going out for a date night when Lorena was about two. Mom and Dad were going to watch the kids, and we were going to Mike's favorite seafood restaurant. We both dressed up and drove laughing like normal to the restaurant. We were sitting in the lobby, and a little girl about Lorena's age came toddling around the chairs. She was adorable in her curls and pink jumper with cute matching pink shoes, grinning and chattering in toddler speak. My mind instantly compared Lorena to this bubbling little girl. My heart broke, and I began to silently sob. Mike knew without saying a word. He just kept rubbing my arm and asking if I wanted to leave. I shook my head, and we proceeded to the table. The poor waiter took one look at my splotched, tear-smeared face, and I could tell he didn't have a clue how to deal with this particular situation. I think he thought I was upset with the wait or the drinks we had. He was especially kind and attentive, so maybe it wasn't all for nothing.

Many times the triggers are just that innocent. The movie *Father of the Bride* with Steve Martin reduced both Mike and me to tears, especially when he is walking his daughter down the aisle. The crowning of the homecoming queen, mothers and daughters shopping together, cheerleaders at football games, the female leads in the drama productions. All of these events can hit hard. And the "what if" game.

Such horrible words—*what if.* I look at Lorena and think, *What if she was typical?* Would she sing, dance, and act like her brother? She loves to watch sports. Maybe she would have been athletic. Would she have been shy or outgoing? Have lots of friends or one best friend? Be cute and girly or dark and goth? The more I let my mind wander down the "what if" path, the deeper back in that swamp I go. I try not to play that game as much as possible. Again, once in a while, it sideswipes. Sometimes an innocent question from a friend is enough to set it off. "So, what is Lorena up to?" Most of the time I can handle it, but if she is having a difficult period or we are having trouble with a particular behavior, I might fall apart.

That "what if" game leads to another phase of grieving that Kubler-Ross did not document, and that is guilt. At one of our Early Intervention support meetings, a mother from Family Resources came to speak to us. The one comment she made to me that really stuck is that when you have a child, the moment they leave the womb, all this guilt gets sucked in. I mean, we all know nature abhors a vacuum, so something had to take up the space. And each of my children was over nine pounds at birth, so there was a lot of womb to fill. Guilt plagued me in those early years. Mike was plagued with that guilt as well.

I constantly thought about my pregnancy and what could have caused this to happen. Was it my fault? And Mike often shared his fears that it was somehow his fault. I clearly remember one time when a study came out about the effects of aspartame in soda and pregnancy. I am addicted to Diet Pepsi and drink it in large quantities. Mike casually asked one day after watching the news, "Do you think it might have been the Diet Pepsi?" I was livid. How dare he point fingers at me, while the same time I was overwhelmed with guilt that maybe that was it. (Disclaimer: there is no proven link between aspartame and autism that I have seen or read about.)

My guilt overwhelmed me when I read about special schools or therapies that were proving successful that we did not have access to or could not afford. I felt guilty if I took time for myself, sure that every moment away from her was somehow not productive for Lorena. I would read about mothers who devoted every minute of every day working with their children. More guilt when I went to work or took time for Mickey or selfishly for myself or didn't devote that time like those mothers did. Then I would feel guilty when I was spending time with her that I was not paying attention to Mike or Mickey.

I learned, though, that *guilt is a useless emotion*. We can only do what we are capable of doing or deciding with what we have at that moment. Do I have regrets? Yes, because I think if Lorena was born today some of her skills might be more fully developed because of the progress in the treatment of autism, but I have also learned that with autism there are no time limits. Lorena grows and develops every day, so if I waste time on regrets and guilt, I miss the opportunity now.

That is the dark side of what if; there is a more upbeat version. I think about how my life would be if Lorena were not autistic from a different viewpoint. I have learned that the world is not all about me. And that is a huge lesson in today's world of entitlement. I am learning patience, although I think that will be a lifelong lesson probably never truly attained. I believe my relationships with friends and family are deep and meaningful because I learned early what was important—people, not things. I value communication and believe I can communicate today at the level I do because of Lorena. Would I be what I am today if she were normal? Would I have learned these lessons? It is a thought-provoking perspective.

I have always thought people who have a well-developed sense of humor and are optimists enjoy life more. It is not that they have fewer troubles or are superficial, but they just have better coping mechanisms. I think I always possessed both those traits. And nurses are known for their sick senses of humor—how else would we deal with all those body fluids and human fragility every day? But believe me, our sense of humor as a family has a whole new level.

For instance, Lorena loves dolls that talk. My brother, Michael, and his wife, Anita, indulged this one Christmas by gifting her with twin talking dolls. They were adorable boy and girl dolls who sat in side-by-side strollers and talked to each other. "I love you," they would chatter back and forth. "You're my brother." "You're my sister." "We have fun." They drove me crazy. Mike and I kept telling Michael and Anita that we were going to call them at two in the morning so they could listen to the dolls' endless verbal exchange. Lorena received these dolls during her hair-pulling phase. Soon, the twins were bald. I figured, better the dolls than her own hair, and let it go. Michael and Anita were visiting one day and happened to see the twins with plucked heads in their strollers. He looked at me and exclaimed, "Oh my God, when did the twins have chemo?" I thought that was hysterical. I would have preferred she pull their voice boxes out.

And probably if we didn't laugh, we would just cry. I have found that time truly is the great healer, giving us perspective. I know how many behaviors we have dealt with, how many milestones we have missed, how many obstacles we have had to overcome or adapt to, and I know that we have found a way to cope with every one of them. Remember that eclipse? The lesson is to *take it piece by piece until the whole doesn't blind you; it just sheds light on your world.*

Playing the Odds

I have mentioned before that Mike, my husband, is not Catholic. We went to see the priest for our marriage counseling meeting. As we began to discuss the ceremony, the priest took the opportunity to tell us that we had a 50 percent greater chance of getting divorced because we were having a "mixed" marriage, since Mike wasn't Catholic. How reassuring. And let me tell you, that really made Mike have warm, fuzzy feelings about the Catholic Church. So if 50 percent of all couples in America get divorced, and we had another 50-percent chance, that put us at 75 percent. Then we were told a few years later that parents of a child with disability have a 75-percent chance of getting divorced.

Now, algebra was never my strong suit, so I don't know where we are at percentage wise. And that doesn't add in our other differences. Mike is a huge procrastinator; I have it done yesterday. I think it comes from all my years as a critical care nurse. Mike will even say to me when I am nagging him about something not being done, "Kim, we don't all work in an ICU." Mike listens to Kiss to relax; I like Enya. His idea of dressing up is a clean T-shirt with his jeans; mine involves heels. I am almost embarrassed to admit the next difference, and it is almost a deal breaker. I am almost horrified to even write it. Mike is a Republican. I know, take a deep breath. I've worked through it; you can too. The reality, though, is that we have finally decided that it is all a crapshoot and we are playing the odds.

That is the humorous take on it, but every marriage has its ups and downs with the normal flow of life—children, work, bills, and general chaos. Add in a child with a disability and all its accompanying drama, and the situation, bluntly, is a strain that can make or break a marriage. I often think it is not the child, the disability, or even the care, but the inability of the parents to support each other that causes the break.

I have described that a parent grieves the loss of the normal child. I think what happens in a marriage is that each person grieves and copes differently. I felt as though Mike was in denial a lot longer than I was, and it made me angry that he would not wake up, admit the problem, and help me figure out how to fix it. When I look back, I realize that I was reacting like the nurse I was. Nurses gather data to assess the situation, look at all the facts, decide on interventions, implement those interventions, and evaluate if they worked, then start the whole cycle all over again until the patient's issues are resolved. This process gave me a tangible way to approach the problem.

However, Mike never went to nursing school. He didn't have a process. He only had what he knew. And what he knew was that his baby girl was not well. This fact made him sad. He had not been taught how to problem-solve medical issues the way I had. This meant he had no way to know how to approach her symptoms. And forget hypothesizing diagnoses. He didn't have a clue what possible pediatric diagnosis we should look at.

Remember, I was really good at being mad. Mike became one of my handy targets. I can be insightful today about why he felt helpless, but at the time I was just mad that he was not doing anything constructive and the decisions all seemed to be falling to me. I also stopped appreciating his quirky sense of humor. How dare he keep teasing and joking when we were in a crisis!

Because we were approaching this so differently, we didn't support each other very well. We became two people battling for our daughter, often against each other. Sometimes I think we are still married in spite of ourselves, because there were times we certainly did not work at the marriage. And sometimes I think we made it because we were so tired of people telling us we weren't going to make it; we were going to show them!

I do know that we have now been married twenty-two years. Today I can say to Mike, "I am tired of making decisions; make this one." He can tell me he is sad. And we can laugh together. We recognize that we still have many rough patches ahead. We have learned, though, that *sometimes you just need to hang tough and not give up, even when all the odds are against you.*

For instance, I recognize that children are not the only ones who reach developmental milestones. Marriages have developmental milestones. We all know that the first year is the honeymoon year. Then generally people move on to the children and career years, where your focus shifts to those activities. Your entire schedule revolves around the kids' school calendar and activities, in addition to your work schedule. At least that is what happened in this home. With Mickey in college and Lorena turning nineteen, we should be in the empty-nest phase. We should be able to go out to dinner alone, go to events without worrying about a sitter, start to be a couple again, run around the house naked when we feel like it. That is not our reality. We have a child that cannot be left alone and who is not leaving anytime soon. And we could run around naked probably without her noticing, but it just wouldn't be appropriate.

The only way we are going to get to the couple phase is to make the hard decision to place Lorena in a group home. That decision is one of those eclipse moments. The idea of choosing where she would live, the day-to-day concern for her well-being, the guilt of not caring for her daily, and the anxiety with knowing we won't see her every day to know she is okay is beyond what I can handle mentally right now. I can't even bring myself to send her to camp overnight right now. I do know that given our history, I will probably be ready for this next step first. I know that this decision will be the healthiest choice for her at some point, but... not yet.

Our relationship is not the only one affected by Lorena's diagnosis. Our son is the other one affected by autism. Our relationship with him is different, I think, than it would have been if Lorena had been typical. I actually think this is one of those positives in the "what if" game.

I had done a clinical rotation at a pediatric hospital during nursing school. I had seen families cope with devastating illness. The well children were often not given their fair share of attention or did not have their needs met. These parents often did not have a choice, since they traveled and stayed away from home so their children could get appropriate care.

I made a decision early that Mickey would have as much of our time as possible. I wanted him to have his own strengths recognized and developed. That is why he went to preschool at a time when it was still optional for the majority of children. Lorena went to her school (therapy), and Mickey went to his. We quickly learned that he loved singing and music. He begged for guitar lessons, so when he was seven we purchased a guitar and he went to weekly lessons. He participated in all those city sports leagues. We couldn't always attend together, but someone was always there to watch. My mom and dad often stepped in as the official "watchers" or chauffeur.

I don't think Lorena's development delays really hit home for him, though, until he was school age. Since Lorena was the second child, he never had that typical sibling relationship that most kids do. Our normal was the normal he expected. Once he entered elementary school and began visiting other homes, he began to realize our situation was not the typical. We made sure that he had a space for his friends to visit and play so they felt welcome in our home too. And we had to teach him how to deal with his peers the first time they met Lorena. We found that blunt honesty was the best way to handle it. I can honestly say that Mickey's friends were incredible, and I don't ever recall any of them ostracizing or making fun of him or her.

He finally figured out that sports were not his game, so to speak. His talent was on the stage. He is a frequent cast and crew member at our local community theatre and by the time he entered college had participated in over twenty productions. The wonderful part of his participation in the theatre is the fact that Lorena enjoys watching him in the productions. This took sitting through several plays in parts, but she finally is to the point where she can sit through an entire production. In fact, Mickey was Cogsworth in our teen theatre production of *Beauty and the Beast*, so when Lorena watches the film, she always points at the clock and identifies it as her brother.

I also think he has learned many lessons. He is helpful. I can still see him holding Lorena's hand when they were toddlers going carefully down the stairs. He still buckles her seat belt for her. On the other hand, he also is a typical brother and draws the line. One day I asked him to assist her in putting on her socks. He threw them at her and said, "She can do it herself."

"Mickey," I scolded, "don't you be mean." I was angry that he would not help her, until I looked and saw that she was putting them on herself. Okay, maybe we do coddle her a little.

He is not judgmental or prejudiced, having learned how painful that can be. He speaks out when things are not right. He can be selfish with his time or talent, saying no when he feels overscheduled, a trait many adults never successfully learn. He is often complimented on his maturity. I personally think the best lesson is the special bond we have. I can honestly say that he still likes to hang with me … most of the time. He has even managed to drag me onto the stage with him.

I think Lorena has taught us that we are what is important—not the house, not the stuff we own. We learned how *to be a better family—less self-centered, more focused on what really matters, and better able to cope with the bad and good life brings.*

Danger, Will Robinson!

Lost in Space was a favorite show of my brother's when we were children. The show featured a family exploring outer space. The son, Will, was a child genius who was accompanied on his adventures by his robot. What I remember from the show is that every time Will would head for trouble, the robot frantically waved its giant metal, clawed arms and warned in a mechanical voice, "Danger, Will Robinson; danger." I relate to this often in my life with Lorena. I find that I am constantly on alert, looking for danger. The danger comes in two forms: emotional and physical.

We, as human beings, tend to like the status quo and don't usually embrace change. When change happens, as it inevitably does, we feel exposed, vulnerable. We tend to cling to what we know, our normal. This was certainly the way I reacted when faced with our situation. We confined ourselves to our home at first with Lorena's illness. The around-the-clock breathing treatments, the frequent trips to therapy, doctors, and all our other responsibilities weren't very conducive to nights out. I felt safer at home. When we left the house, we had to face all those well-meaning questions about how well she was or was not doing. I have never quite figured out how to answer when someone asks, "And how is Lorena doing?" in that patient, quiet tone usually reserved for visitation lines at the funeral home. When she was younger, I would give a detailed report on her progress, daring the person to take away my belief that she was going to reach normal soon. Nowadays, I just say, "Fine," when I want to humorously reply, "Well, still autistic." Of course, I might think that is funny; they probably would think I was being really inappropriate.

Lorena did get stronger, the breathing treatments stopped, the visits to the doctors got less frequent, but a new behavior began to emerge. The meltdown. Every time Lorena was in a new situation or with new people, she would scream and cry, often hitting her head. She was inconsolable, and the only way the behavior decreased was to remove her from the situation. We didn't understand at the time that in these situations there was a stimulus that was intolerable for her. I have already written that church was one of these areas. To be honest, at first, it was anywhere that wasn't home. And sometimes home wasn't even okay.

I always say that Lorena became attached to my hip very early in her life. I had one school official tell me that he thought parents of children with disabilities have an extra-long umbilical cord that doesn't get cut as soon as normal children. That is probably true. I can confirm that Lorena would not even go to Mike or my mom early in her life. I know that it was miserable for both of them and any sitter when I left for work. Many nights I would go to work with her uncontrollable shrieking and crying the last thing I heard walking out the door. When she finally could walk, I would walk out not only to the noise but with her little body plastered to the door, her face splotchy, and tears streaking down her cheeks.

I was her mother, had given birth to her, stayed with her as much as possible in the hospital, and taken her to therapy and her appointments. While Mike had been there with me, I think instinctively she knew that I was the one who had carried her inside me and had never quite cut that cord.

These meltdowns didn't just happen when I went to work; they happened if we went to a restaurant and I went to the restroom. They happened if we went to visit at someone's home and I left the room. They basically happened anytime she thought I was leaving her.

I can't begin to tell you how emotionally drained I was every time I went out the door. I felt so guilty for leaving her and for leaving whoever was caring for her with this screaming child. I would arrive at work or the store or an appointment barely able to concentrate. It took every bit of my energy to focus on where I was at and not just sit down to cry with sadness, guilt, and angry frustration.

The meltdowns also happened in church, although with time, less acutely in the grocery store, at friend and families' homes, at the park, in therapy, and many other events. I remember her second Thanksgiving, when we went to my grandpa's house. She began to shriek as soon as we sat down at the table. I picked her and her plate up and walked into the living room. She and I had Thanksgiving dinner on the floor of the living room. While my family sat at the table, laughing and visiting, I cried while trying to feed mashed potatoes to my tearful child.

I have to admit, I was irrationally angry at her for ruining the holiday while at the same time sad that she could not enjoy our extended family. I was a typical wife ticked at her typical husband, who couldn't figure out that I would have liked it if he had taken Lorena into the living room. (Remember, I just wrote that she would scream if I left the room, but I said I was irrationally angry, didn't I?) My aunt did offer to hold her while I went to the table for a while. I just said no, wallowing in my self-pity.

We began to refuse invitations and limit our trips away from home. I have said we were exhausted from all that had occurred, and add to that a child who had a meltdown every time we went somewhere, and it just didn't seem worth the effort to go anywhere. Plus, when we did go to a restaurant or store and she did have a meltdown, we got the angry stares and mutters. I knew they were thinking: *Why doesn't she do something with that child? What kind of parents are they?*

It might be a big, wide world, but ours narrowed considerably. Emotionally, Lorena seemed only safe in ours. We also felt safest here. No explanations, no stares, limited meltdowns. Looking back now, I can admit that this was part of our denial. We assured ourselves that we would find out what was wrong and then once it was "fixed," we would go back to our normal activities.

We didn't become complete recluses, though. As I have related earlier, Lorena did go to therapy three times a week. The therapy took place at a local rehab hospital, where the patients ranged in age from teenagers to senior citizens. The therapists had just begun to accept pediatric patients. I would hand her over to the therapist, and she would begin to cry. I could not watch the therapy or be anywhere that she could see me, or the meltdown would escalate. The therapist usually spent a good portion of each therapy session calming Lorena down. I had noticed at home, though, that music seemed to settle her, so I began to bring a small child's CD player, and her therapist would play her favorite Disney soundtracks, which seemed to capture her attention enough to stop the meltdown. Gradually, over months, she didn't melt down and would cooperate.

I have already detailed going to church, but breakfast at the restaurant after was another place she would melt down. We went to a local restaurant for breakfast after Mass. She would cry, arch her back, and rock her whole body. We would play music with a headset, bring her favorite dolls or books, and try to talk her down. A few times, she scooted off the chair and would sit under the table. She would hold her dolls, look at her books, and settle down. I kept dragging her up, and she would start to melt down again. Eventually, I decided it just didn't matter if she was sitting down there. She was okay, at peace, and I got to eat breakfast.

Each new place was a similar challenge. I entered every new place on full alert, scoping out the area for any possible danger or triggers that might upset Lorena. We learned and she matured. We learned that the most dangerous places were the ones that contained the items she was compulsive about. For instance, she loved to watch videos. They were a great distraction for her. And there wasn't a video machine she couldn't figure out how to work. However, in the true way of those with autism, she would wind and rewind the tape, watching a scene or clip over and over. The video and VCR both suffered from this treatment. Every time we went to friends, family, or anyone's home, she would begin to tear apart their video collections and their VCRs. If we halted the behavior—and we did—a major meltdown would occur.

They would assure us it was fine, but I was afraid she would ruin the collection or VCR. It seemed easier just to choose not to go in the first place or to leave.

In addition, she displayed this behavior with books, dolls, and Game Boys. We bought her a Game Boy. This worked well, but part of her meltdowns was biting—books, dolls, and any other object she was holding. Thank God it didn't extend to people. She bit and broke the screen on numerous Game Boys.

Then there were the meltdowns in stores when she wanted an item and we said "no." Or the ones in McDonald's when it was the wrong week for the toy she desired in the Happy Meal. Or the ones when we didn't have a clue what was wrong. Those meltdowns were in places we went to all the time. Forget about going to the movie theater.

This particular aspect of autism is probably the most difficult. We have learned many coping tools over the years. The most important coping tool is for me to stay calm. In the early years, the more she wound up, the more I did. My entire body would tense, I would become tearful, my voice would pitch higher, and I would hype up trying to calm her down. She would pick up on this, and it would increase the behavior. I have now learned that I need to stay calm, keep my voice normal, and my body language relaxed. Just doing that goes a long way to beginning to settle her down. Basically, what was the worst thing that was going to happen? People would stare and whisper. Been there, done that. And as I told Mickey when I was trying to help him cope with this behavior, "What are they going to do, take your birthday away?"

I learned to go prepared. Hence, the goodie bag. The goodie bag is a bag we take with us to everything. I would pack her favorite items—dolls, Game Boy, books. She would always have a distraction no matter where she went. We pack sensory integration items such as special toys and hand vibrators or massagers, which help to settle her.

We learned to take favorite food and drinks. Many children with autism develop very particular food tastes. This is beyond being just a picky eater. We went through a period of time where the only thing she would eat was bologna. And I mean only: she ate bologna for breakfast, lunch, dinner, and snacks. We tried to feed her some vegetables and other items. Occasionally we could sneak another food in, but not often. Then came the chicken nugget phase, then the spaghetti phase. These food obsessions occur for multiple reasons, such as tactile sensitivity, which can cause resistance to certain textures, tastes, or temperatures of food, or just obsessive behavior. Gradually, although she would concentrate on one item, her food tolerances and preferences expanded. Today her diet is a more balanced one.

I had a family tell me at a support group meeting that the only meal their child would eat was chicken nuggets, corn, and French fries. The problem was that the chicken nuggets and fries were easy and on most menus; the corn was not. I recommended they just take corn with them in a thermos all the time. It was the easiest way to prevent the meltdown. So their goodie bag needed to include the corn. And if a restaurant was not friendly when they pulled the corn out, then it did not need their business.

The goodie bag has spawned one of the funniest Lorena incidents. She is old enough now to pack her own bag. I just tell her before we leave to get her stuff together. I don't check what is in there. Well, we arrived at church one week, and she was being really quiet and good. Pleased, I look down to praise her, and to my dismay, she had a Victoria's Secret catalog and apparently was quite interested in a red push-up bra. I tried to flip the pages back to the nightgowns, but, in typical Lorena style, she was totally focused on the red bra page. I finally gave up because it was making more of a ruckus to fight over the magazine than to let her look at it. The next week when we went to church, my dad instructed that I "make sure she doesn't have that book this week."

The goodie bag presents another dilemma. She steals. If I notice we are somewhere and she won't let go of the bag, I can assume she has pilfered an item. This particular behavior has two difficulties. One, I know she is going to have a meltdown as soon as I remove the item. Yet it is important she knows this behavior is not acceptable. Two, when friends, families, and even strangers realize what is going on, I typically am told, "Oh, let her have it. She doesn't know the difference." Yeah, right. If she knows to hide it in her bag, she knows she shouldn't have it. And although most of the time in a home it is a relatively cheap item, like a book or video, I don't want her to do this in a store. I know, though, that people are just trying to be kind, and I appreciate the thought, but it doesn't help what we are trying to teach her. I also realize that friends and family were trying to make us more comfortable by excusing her behavior. However, with a child with autism, you have to be very careful. If you allow a behavior once, they never forget and will repeat the behavior. We have to be very careful with setting the standard and sticking to it.

I know people are truly not sure how to react. I think back to when I was young. I hardly saw people with handicaps. The mentally and physically challenged were mostly sequestered in institutions and private homes. The general public was not exposed to all the behaviors and adaptations families had to make. Today, though, with the help of the

American Disabilities Act, we see everyone of every ability everywhere. I think that it should be this way. I realize that this has many implications.

When we go out to eat we are just trying to enjoy a meal out in a restaurant, and I realize that is what other families and couples are also trying to accomplish. We have all read the frequent Dear Abby columns in regards to children being disruptive in restaurants and ruining diners' pleasure. And while I understand their feelings, I have learned if I take her out of every situation, I never teach her how to adapt to these new situations. Somehow Mike and I have to help her adapt while still being respectful to others. There are times we choose not to go somewhere based on her behavior that day.

I remember one time we were going to my brother's for a picnic. Lorena had been having a rough day, so on the way out to his house I said to her, "Now, you are going to be a good girl." She emphatically shook her head and said no. I repeated, "You will behave." She again said no. Well, let me tell you. She lived up to her word and was horrible. I don't even remember if we ate or not. After a short interval, I just apologized and hauled her butt home. She cried the whole way home. I told her that if she wanted to stay, she needed to behave.

I recognize that Lorena has days where she is just a typical child acting out, and there are times when she is truly having a meltdown. I have been with her long enough to know the difference. Lorena loves to go to our high school football games. There is an entire ritual that occurs when we go. We have to buy a program as soon we enter the gates. Then we have to buy a bottle of water, and we always sit in the same row in the same section at the game (although that is due to Grandpa, not Lorena).

One day I took Lorena for a ride on her special bike. The junior varsity football team was playing, and she wanted to stop and watch. The problem began, though, as soon as we walked into the gate because they don't have programs, and the next issue was they don't sell concessions. She began to cry and hit her head. I tried to talk her through it without luck. I couldn't get her to leave, though, and she was now the same height as I was, so it wasn't just a matter of carrying her out anymore. We went up to the stands, but she kept signing for a program and water and escalating terribly when I kept explaining there were none. I finally got her to leave, but by the time we got to her bike, she was shrieking, hitting her head, and shaking all over. Suddenly she took a shuddering breath, grabbed my hand, and rubbed my cheek. She kept looking me in the eye and nodding.

I understood her more at that moment than I ever had. I could see on her face that she was embarrassed by her outburst. She was trying to apologize in the best way she could. My heart went out to her. I always knew she could not control her outbursts, but that episode truly showed me how the autism controlled her reactions.

I will say that the older Lorena gets, the fewer the meltdowns. The meltdowns do not last nearly as long. She transitions to new places easier, often just exploring the area and then sitting down with her goodie bag to entertain herself.

People often ask me if there is not a medication that would help her. She is on a medication for anxiety, but it doesn't cure all of it. In addition, I am very cautious with medications. I would find when we went to support groups that the kids with autism would have a huge list of traditional and herbal medications. I would ask the parents, "What do these do for your child? Do you see a difference?" Many times they would not be able to detail any difference. It made me wonder why they were on them then. We tried medicine on and off with Lorena—for sleep and anxiety. They all have multiple side effects, and I was concerned. My bottom line with medication is to choose the least amount, and if I don't see a positive outcome, then I don't use it.

As parents, this is another area of concern and safety. I often read about children receiving many questionable treatments with no research basis for the treatment. I believe there are two reasons for this. One, some health-care providers—traditional or non-traditional—are not as ethical as they should be. They take advantage-promoting treatments that often have no proof of helping our children. And we, as parents, grasp at every straw trying to find that cure.

An example that comes to mind is several years ago the drug Secretin received attention because a mother detailed her child's miraculous recovery from autism after receiving the drug for treatment of a gastrointestinal condition. There was a rush from parents to doctors to get the drug prescribed. Drug production could not keep up with demand. I was one of the first in line.

I distinctly remember my conversation with my family physician about this treatment. He said, "It's just a hormone and can't hurt, so I think you can safely try it." And we did. Did we have an outcome? She did sleep through the night after that. Was it a result of the drug? Coincidence? Development? I don't know. I recognize that subsequent treatments yielded no measurable results. I learned an important lesson from that experience. *Lorena's treatments needed to be based on research-evidenced options, be continued only if they resulted in an outcome, and in addition, I needed to make sure they would not harm.* The no harm came from the fact that at the same time the Secretin story broke, I began to hear about other treatments that actually had resulted in death.

Even with her decreased meltdowns, I am still on high alert. I don't think people understand that no matter how far she has progressed, I cannot leave her in a strange room unsupervised. Either Mike or I have to be present at all times to make sure her needs are met or that she doesn't encounter any danger.

In fact, sometimes she gets in trouble even when we are sitting right there. We went to a wedding when she was about three. She had just started walking. She looked so pretty in her dress, toddling around the table. I kept one eye on her and the other watching people enjoy themselves, until suddenly I noticed she wasn't just aimlessly toddling around the table. She was community drinking. She was going from cup to cup and sipping the beer that people had left on the table. I told my mom, "Oh, great, not only is she autistic, but she is an alcoholic too!"

Which is the second part of our Will Robinson scenario. Lorena is not aware of most of the physical dangers in her environment. For instance, she will walk right out into the street. We moved into town when Lorena was five. One of the first days we were in the house, she opened the door and walked out. She had never been able to open the screen door before and suddenly acquired the skill while I was upstairs for a moment. When I came down, she was gone. Hysterical, Mickey and I (Mike was at work) ran out calling her name. We found her down the street, where a kindly neighbor was holding her by the arm and asking her repeatedly what her name was and where she lived. Lorena was giggling and twirling, obviously not answering. I thanked the neighbor profusely and explained the situation. I thought, "Oh, great introduction to the neighborhood." We installed alarms on the doors, sort of like the ding-dong ones you hear when you go into a store. I felt safer.

We have a lot of these moments. I call them the "Oh, that's great, uh-oh" moments. We encourage and work with her to acquire new skills, but on the other hand, every new skill has a flip side, which could be dangerous. And sometimes just downright messy. She learned to open the refrigerator and then threw a dozen eggs down our carpeted stairs. The therapist, who was helping her learn the pincer grasp to pick items up, taught her by pulling Kleenex out of the pop-up Kleenex box. We found shredded tissue all over our backyard and home for years. I won't even discuss the smeared food after the preschool decided to use different puddings as a paint medium for a project one day.

While I don't like cleaning up tissue or pudding or eggs, I can handle that. I fear for Lorena's physical well-being. I can't teach her stranger danger. I can't be there every moment to make sure someone doesn't take advantage of her at school or other events she is attending with different groups. I do the best I can to make her environment safe, but sometimes I don't even realize the extent of the danger.

Lorena was a toddler when she ended up in ICU after pouring Lysol into a cup of milk and drinking it. I had brought down the cleaning supplies one Saturday morning. The cleaning supplies were locked in a closet in a sealed container. I decided to have one more cup of coffee and read the paper before I started my weekly cleaning. Suddenly, I caught a whiff of pine. I got up, suspicious, and followed the odor. She had poured the cleaner in her cup and was swirling it, watching the bubbles. I thought maybe she didn't drink it, but one whiff of her breath proved that theory wrong. I called poison control, not completely sure what to do. They instructed me to take her right to the hospital, where they pumped her stomach and put her in the unit. Even knowing the cleaner was poisonous, I didn't realize it actually could cause kidney failure or death. I was scared down to the bone.

I was scared down to the bone too the many times she choked on food. She does not have size perception. For instance, she will try to put Barbie clothes on a regular size doll, never realizing they won't fit. This size-perception issue extends to food. She will put huge bites into her mouth and then not properly chew. We have to cut everything up and to this day, encourage her to chew carefully. I can't count the number of times I did the Heimlich. The worst was the day she choked on a piece of hamburger. She was turning blue and not breathing when I began to do the Heimlich. I screamed at Mike, "Call 911! To which he responded, "I don't know the number." I yelled, "9-1-1." He just looked at me blankly. Finally, I said, "Call the operator; dial 0." By the time the operator answered, I had cleaned her throat. Terrified, I sat on the floor and started to bawl. Again, he is not an ICU nurse and in his panic could not even remember how to dial 9-1-1.

You must be thinking, *What could she possibly learn from all this?* I learned *when you have no control and are scared, it can be totally freeing.* We spend our entire lives afraid—afraid of what will happen or what others will say. I learned that this fear prevents us from becoming all that we can be or doing what we dream of doing. I stopped worrying about what others think or letting it limit me, and suddenly I found a freedom I didn't realize existed. I can try anything. Succeed at everything, no. But I can try to do anything that I really want to. And since I don't have society's rule book playing in my head, thanks to Lorena, I don't worry about failing. Who really cares if I fail? I know that in failure, I learn and grow. That is what matters, not what "they" think.

The result is that I try new things, like getting up on a stage in front of hundreds of strangers or speaking out when I feel strongly. This newfound freedom helped me get my master's degree in nursing, take on new roles at work, run for school board (I lost the election, but I tried), and expose myself by writing a book. You see, the worst thing I can imagine happened: my child has struggles I never wanted her to face. And when your worst fear is realized, what is there left to fear?

The Road Not Taken

Robert Frost wrote in his 1920 poem about the road in the woods not taken. He talked of standing at the fork in the road and having to choose which to take. He also spoke of the debate in choosing one road over the other and what each could hold. Lastly, he describes how the choice of road can make all the difference in a life.

I did not choose the road I travel. Often, Lorena drags me down it unwillingly. At times, I envision traveling down the other road, the road of normal. I think that trip may be easier, but I am no longer convinced it is better. I think we have found the better in each other and ourselves on this path. I am convinced that I live a better life, one filled with friends, family, love, and joy.

References

1. Trapp "U.S. uninsured total again tops 46 million" *amednews.com* September 21, 2009 Web January 28, 2010 (http://www.ama-assn.org/amednews/2009/09/21/gvsa0921.html)

2. Autism Speaks "Autism speaks announces multistate insurance legislation campaign" *Autism Speaks* Web April 22, 2009 (http://www.autismspeaks.org/government_affairs/state_issues.php)

3. Autism Speaks "What is autism?" *Autism Speaks* Web April 22, 2009 (http://www.autismspeaks.org/whatisit/index.php)

4. The National Fragile X Foundation "What is Fragile X" Web April 22, 2009 (http://www.fragilex.org/html/what.htm)

5. NIDCD "Autism and Communication" *National Institute on Deafness and Other Communication Disorders* Web April 22, 2009 (http://www.nidcd.nih.gov/health/voice/autism.asp)

6. NIDCD "American Sign Language" *National Institute on Deafness and Other Communication Disorders* Web April 22, 2009 (http://www.nidcd.nih.gov/health/hearing/asl.asp)

7. Stewart, R. "Should we insist on eye contact with people who have Autism Spectrum Disorders" *Indiana Resource Center for Autism* Web April 22, 2009 (http://www.iidc.indiana.edu/irca/Sensory/insisteyecontact.html)

8. The National Fragile X Foundation "Tactile Defensiveness" Web April 22, 2009 (http://www.fragilex.org/html/tactile.htm)

9. The National Autistic Society "Sleep and Autism: Helping Your Child" Web April 22, 2009   (http://www.nas.org.uk/nas/jsp/polopoly.jsp?a=3376&d=1071)

10. Pardini, Priscilla "The history of special education" *Rethinking Schools Online* Web April 22, 2009 (http://www.rethinkingschools.org/archive/16_03/Hist163.shtml)

11. Martin, E. Martin, R. & Terman, D. "The legislative and litigation history of special education" *The Future of Children* Web April 22, 2009 (http://www.princeton.edu/futureofchildren/publications/journals/article/index.xml?journalid=57&articleid=338)

12. Hobdell, E. Chronic Sorrow and Depression in Parents of Children with Neural Tube Defects. *Journal of Neuroscience Nursing* 36(2) p. 82.